Nags Headers

"History is only as real
as memories, and I have
stored volumes behind my
eyes."

Tim McLaurin,
The River Less Run

E. R. Outlaw, Sr. Cottage

Spider Villa

Lamb-Martin-Stewart-
Folk-Patterson Cottage

Pailin-Skinner Cottage

FACING PAGE:
AERIAL VIEW OF THE UNPAINTED ARISTOCRACY
Photo by Drew Crawford Wilson
Photos above by Drew Crawford Wilson

Nags Headers

SUSAN BYRUM ROUNTREE

JOHN F. BLAIR, PUBLISHER   Winston-Salem, North Carolina

Published by John F. Blair, Publisher

*The paper in this book meets the guidelines
for permanence and durability of the
Committee on Production Guidelines for
Book Longevity of the Council on Library Resources.*

Library of Congress Cataloging-in-Publication Data

Rountree, Susan Byrum, 1957–
Nags Headers / by Susan Byrum Rountree.
p.   cm.
Includes bibliographical references and index.
ISBN 0-89587-239-0 (hardcover: alk. paper)—ISBN 0-89587-240-4
(pbk.: alk. paper)   1. Nags Head (N.C.)—History. 2. Nags Head
(N.C.—Biography. 3. Interviews—North Carolina—Nags Head.
4. Oral history. 5. Nags Head (N.C.)—History—Pictorial works.
6. Cottages—North Carolina—Nags Head. I. Title.

F264.N3 R68 2001
975.6'175—dc21
20011035244

Design by Debra Long Hampton

FACING PAGE:

A SEA OAT MAKES ITS MARK.

Photo by Drew Crawford Wilson

For my parents,
who gave me a place to love,
and for Rick, who always believes
I can write the story,
even when I don't believe it myself

Contents

Facing page:

An old conch guards the steps

Photo by Drew Crawford Wilson

AUTHOR'S NOTE

*I*T IS IN MEMORY that we find our truth, our individual history. The truth of Nags Head can be found most easily in the stories Nags Headers store behind their eyes. So much of what is rich about Nags Head lives in the memories shared by those who know it best.

There are times when those recollections collide with each other and with historic fact. When fact could be corroborated with memory, I have done so. Otherwise, the truth of each story lay with the teller.

This is a story of memory, of houses that shelter not only the people who live in them but also the stories that bring the soul of the place to life.

A WEATHERVANE ON AN OLD GARAGE

Photo by Drew Crawford Wilson

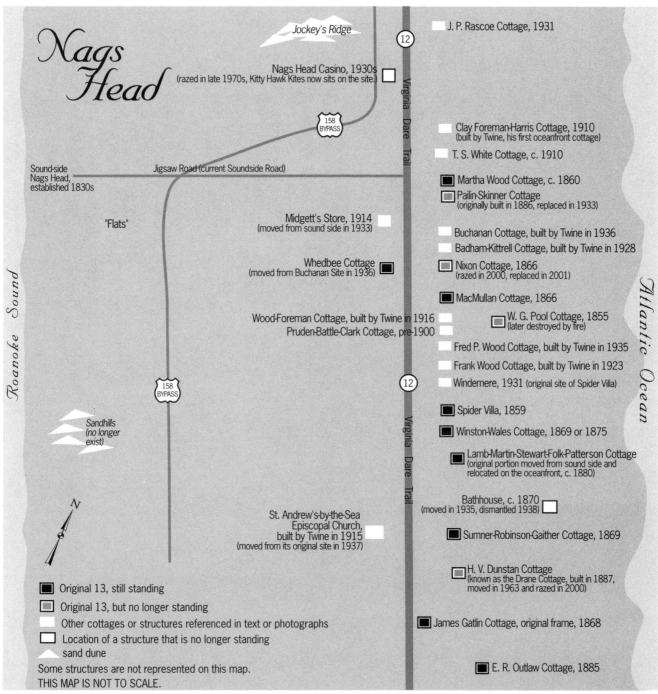

Nags Head

Jockey's Ridge

Nags Head Casino, 1930s
(razed in late 1970s, Kitty Hawk Kites now sits on the site.)

158 BYPASS

Sound-side Nags Head, established 1830s

Jigsaw Road (current Soundside Road)

"Flats"

Midgett's Store, 1914
(moved from sound side in 1933)

Whedbee Cottage
(moved from Buchanan Site in 1936)

Wood-Foreman Cottage, built by Twine in 1916
Pruden-Battle-Clark Cottage, pre-1900

158 BYPASS

Sandhills
(no longer exist)

St. Andrew's-by-the-Sea
Episcopal Church,
built by Twine in 1915
(moved from its original site in 1937)

N

Roanoke Sound

12

Virginia Dare Trail

J. P. Rascoe Cottage, 1931

Clay Foreman-Harris Cottage, 1910
(built by Twine, his first oceanfront cottage)

T. S. White Cottage, c. 1910

Martha Wood Cottage, c. 1860

Pailin-Skinner Cottage
(originally built in 1886, replaced in 1933)

Buchanan Cottage, built by Twine in 1936

Badham-Kittrell Cottage, built by Twine in 1928

Nixon Cottage, 1866
(razed in 2000, replaced in 2001)

MacMullan Cottage, 1866

W. G. Pool Cottage, 1855
(later destroyed by fire)

Fred P. Wood Cottage, built by Twine in 1935

Frank Wood Cottage, built by Twine in 1923

Windemere, 1931 (original site of Spider Villa)

12

Spider Villa, 1859

Winston-Wales Cottage, 1869 or 1875

Lamb-Martin-Stewart-Folk-Patterson Cottage
(original portion moved from sound side and
relocated on the oceanfront, c. 1880)

Bathhouse, c. 1870
(moved in 1935, dismantled 1938)

Sumner-Robinson-Gaither Cottage, 1869

H. V. Dunstan Cottage
(known as the Drane Cottage, built in 1887,
moved in 1963 and razed in 2000)

Virginia Dare Trail

James Gatlin Cottage, original frame, 1868

E. R. Outlaw Cottage, 1885

Atlantic Ocean

Original 13, still standing

Original 13, but no longer standing

Other cottages or structures referenced in text or photographs

Location of a structure that is no longer standing

sand dune

Some structures are not represented on this map.
THIS MAP IS NOT TO SCALE.

Information courtesy of the North Carolina Division of Archives and History and obtained in part from the National Register of Historic Places Nomination, 1977, on file at the Office of Survey and Planning. Other research by J. Peter Rascoe III. This information is as accurate as could be obtained at publication and may be subject to error.

WATCHING THE WAVES
THE MOST IMMINENT THREAT TO HISTORIC COTTAGE ROW HAS BEEN AND ALWAYS WILL BE THE SEA.
FROM RIGHT: THE WOOD-FOREMAN COTTAGE AND THE PRUDEN-BATTLE-CLARK COTTAGE STAND WATCH OVER THE TIDES.
Photo by Drew Crawford Wilson

> Tide, n. A portion, extent, or space of time; an age, a season; the flowing or swelling of the sea or its alternate rising and falling, twice each lunar day, due to the attraction of the moon and, in a less degree, of the sun; the alternate inflow and outflow produced by this on a coast; the flood and ebb.
>
> *The Oxford English Dictionary*

PROLOGUE

*J*OHN "POSSUM" SILVER stood on the side porch of his mother's Nags Head, North Carolina, beach cottage, watching the sea claw at the front steps. A series of low-pressure systems had plagued the Outer Banks during the first cold weeks of February, and for the third time in less than two weeks, Silver stood by as an angry Atlantic took pieces of the house with each wave.

It was four-thirty in the morning. As the front pilings of the porch began to give way, Silver leaned into the house, stroking it softly. The east side of the roof blew off, but he continued leaning as if he could hold the house up, waiting for low tide.

The Winston-Wales Cottage is a good house, has been in his mother's family for over a hundred years, weathering hurricanes and northeasters like the Ash Wednesday Storm in 1962, when the living room filled with sand.

For the last few years especially, Silver has watched the Nags Head tides rise and fall, the ocean creeping ever closer to his family's legacy. Where once a seventy-five-foot swath of sand stretched between porch and surf at high tide, storm-tide breakers shot up through the floor of the house.

"It was beautiful, but it was bad," recalls Silver of the February 1998 storm, his Southern drawl drifting

A Nags Head nightlight switch, made of a strand of seashells scavanged from the beach, is a common sight inside the Unpainted Aristocracy. This one hangs in the Winston-Wales Cottage.
Photo by Drew Crawford Wilson

of sand and of efforts to preserve the legacy for generations to come.

Possum Silver and those like him are true Nags Headers, families who have lived in this area of North Carolina's Outer Banks since it was settled in the eighteenth century. They're the descendants of those who

Protruding benches, built into the arms of porches, are trademarks of Nags Head builder S. J. Twine's style.
Photo by Drew Crawford Wilson

through the air like cool salt spray. "I had been one of those who said, 'We'll love it while it's here,' but I realized that if something happened to this house, my roots would be gone."

Silver is not alone in having roots that sink deep into the Nags Head sand. This is the story of his legacy and that of other families who helped settle Nags Head, one of North Carolina's oldest beach resorts. It is a beachcomber's tale of life on a beloved stretch

THE FULL-WIDTH DORMER AND PROPPED SHUTTERS OF THE WOOD-FOREMAN COTTAGE ARE EXAMPLES OF S. J. TWINE'S HANDIWORK THAT TYPIFY THE NAGS HEAD STYLE.
Photo by Drew Crawford Wilson

braved the choppy waters of the Albemarle Sound and battled northeasters to fashion small fishing shacks in the area before the Civil War. And they are families, like Silver's, who've held on to this legacy for close to 150 years, preserving a piece of North Carolina's history within their shingled walls.

Nags Headers kick off their shoes at the porch steps, even in winter. They cling to salt air, sand, and sea like children who won't venture far from their mother's skirts. They have never been tourists.

Nags Headers watch from the comfort of their front-porch rockers as the sea shifts the sand. Their legacy grew from those small fishing shacks of scavenged wood into the comfortable, salt-swept cottages that now line the shore.

It is the cottages themselves that define the character of Nags Head more than anything else. Weathered signs on the edge of the "slow road" wave in the sea breeze, touting names like Happy Shack, Dune Swale, and Windemere. These old cottages, christened "the Unpainted Aristocracy" by *Raleigh News and Observer* editor Jonathan Daniels, sit tucked among the dunes, nudging passersby to wonder what life is like behind their rusted screen doors.

SEA OATS IN FRONT OF THE PAILIN-SKINNER COTTAGE
Photo by Drew Crawford Wilson

The Nags Head Beach Cottage Row Historic District—on the National Register of Historic Places since 1977—stretches a mile along the beach, forming a pattern of angles and lines the color of driftwood. Porches wrap the dull gray houses like wide brims on summer hats; shutters propped open like lazy eyelids cast shadows on sand and horizon. Defined by weathered wooden shingles, sweeping gabled roofs, single, full-width dormers, and protruding benches built into the arms of porches, this simple architecture is the patina of Old Nags Head, what old-comers think of first when they see this beach in their mind's eye.

More than five generations have traipsed up the steps and through the halls of the cottages of Nags Head. They combed the giant dunes nearby before paved roads marked the way, settling into a summer life governed only by tides, sea breezes, and the mailboats that docked daily in the Roanoke Sound. They learned to love the calming nature of the Atlantic Ocean, to respect its changing tides and treasure the slow pace of life by the sea.

Family by family, they passed their legacy from grandfathers to granddaughters, from great-granddaughters to sons, ensuring that their familial love of house and beach will continue as long as the houses stand.

As constant as the tides, no matter how the world shifts and moves and changes, this small stretch of sand will always be home for Nags Headers.

From left, the Badham-Kittrell Cottage, the Buchanan Cottage, and the Pailin-Skinner Cottage shelter a century of life at Nags Head.

Photo by Drew Crawford Wilson

Ebb Tide

EARLY NAGS HEADERS PLAY IN THE SURF, C. 1900.

Courtesy of the Outer Banks History Center

I. EBB TIDE: MOVING TOWARD THE SEA, 1860-1915

THE LAND AROUND NAGS HEAD has a place in history as home to North Carolina's earliest natives and a claim to the state's most famous lost citizen—Virginia Dare. This place has long been shrouded in mystery, captivating the imagination of storytellers for centuries.

As early as the sixteenth century, the barrier island that is home to Nags Head—just an hour's drive north of Cape Hatteras—was explored by Indians and Englishmen alike. When the Englishmen first landed here, they found an expanse of sand unlike any they'd ever seen, its towering dunes the size of small mountains gracing the shore. In the mid-1500s, shipwrecked sailors sought the island for shelter, food, and safety. Stories abound of natives greeting ships, of fishing until their canoes were brimming over with catch, of drying the Englishmen's damp clothes over the fires inside their houses. For the most part, the English explorers found these native Carolinians to be gentle and kind.

Though an English colony settled on Roanoke Island in 1587, it vanished soon after the birth of Virginia Dare, the first English child born in the New World. Nags Head itself, home to little save salt and sand and wind, was virtually untouched by civilization until the eighteenth century.

The area's first permanent white families—fishermen and ship salvagers—settled in the 1700s on the Roanoke Sound side of the island halfway between Hatteras and Corolla. Known as "Bankers," they

CHILDREN SIT ON A DORY BOAT IN FRONT OF THE COTTAGE LINE, EARLY 1900S.
THE PRUDEN-BATTLE-CLARK COTTAGE STANDS IN THE BACKGROUND.

Photo courtesy of Fred L. Fearing / Reproduced by Drew Crawford Wilson

scavenged wood from shipwrecks, fashioning one-room shacks over the sound's waters and in the woods near the many large dunes that loomed over the Nags Head landscape.

Many of these fishermen lived in camps, setting their nets in the sea at dusk with dory boats, pulling them to shore at dawn. Their descendants still hold to this practice, fishing along the oceanfront season by season. And many sons of early Nags Headers formed crews for the lifesaving stations scattered up and down the Outer Banks.

Some say Nags Head was christened for a place of the same name on England's coast. But most folks who know the area prefer the tale of pirates who roamed the beaches at night, their only light a lantern tied to the neck of an old nag. Legend contends that ships at sea would mistake the light for the bow of a friendly ship, head toward it, and run aground on one of the many sand bars, becoming easy targets for waiting scavengers.

It was a Perquimans County planter by the name of Francis Nixon who first brought his family to Nags

Head on vacation before the Civil War, unknowingly beginning an unspoken connection between the area's summer families that today's Nags Headers say links them more deeply than blood.

In the early 1830s, the sea and its healing powers drew Nixon and his neighbors—other wealthy planters from nearby Chowan, Bertie, Perquimans, and Pasquotank Counties—to summer at the beach. After the crops were up and growing, plantation owners came to the barrier island to escape the threat of malaria and for the good health encouraged by seawater and salt air. They caught steamers at river docks and carried their children, household slaves, cows, and chickens on their boat ride to the beach.

They found the Bankers there living in the "flats," the wooded area in the middle of the island. A small tourist trade soon sprang up on the banks of the sound, the natives providing horses and carts, fish and fresh vegetables for the tourists. By June 1841, vacationers at Nags Head strolled along a boardwalk that nudged the sound and sipped tea in the parlor of the new Ocean Retreat, a hotel that looked out over the Roanoke Sound. If they wanted to feel the salt air on their faces, they walked no more than a mile from the sound to the Atlantic Ocean on a boardwalk flanked by small huts where bathers changed into and out of their all-wool swimming costumes. Some vacationers built their own cottages on the sand hills.

In 1855, an Elizabeth City doctor by the name of W. G. Pool built an oceanfront house at Nags Head. Pool didn't like the loneliness of beachfront

living, so, in 1866, he gave the Midgett family thirty dollars for fifty acres, then sold the land for a dollar per lot to the wives of his neighbors back home. The first lot sold to Kate Overman, the wife of R. F. Overman of Elizabeth City. She was soon joined by Henrietta Fearing, Florence Grandy, and several others, who would become Pool's neighbors by the sea.

Shingled cottages soon sprang up like sea oats on the Nags Head beach. By 1885, a baker's dozen shacks dotted the sand at the ocean's edge.

Nine of those original thirteen Nags Head cottages survived to greet the twenty-first century. They stand shoulder to shoulder on the southern end of town, rickety wooden reminders of the way things used to be. Their owners hold fast not only to their beloved cottages, but also to their memories of a slower time.

"My grandfather bought this four-room fishing

EARLY NAGS HEADERS ON THE BEACH, C. 1900

Courtesy of the Outer Banks History Center

ARRIVING ON THE SOUND-SIDE WATERFRONT AT NAGS HEAD, C. 1900

Courtesy of the Outer Banks History Center

BOAT ARRIVAL - NAGS HEAD N.C. No 2

NAGS HEAD TOURISTS SHADE THEMSELVES WITH UMBRELLAS AS THEY ARRIVE ON THE SOUND-SIDE DOCK.

Courtesy of the Outer Banks History Center

PATRONS LINE THE PIER OUTSIDE THE OLD HOLLOWELL
HOTEL IN SOUND-SIDE NAGS HEAD. (DATE UNKNOWN)

Photo courtesy of Fred L. Fearing
Reproduced by Drew Crawford Wilson

shack in 1908, the year my mother was five," says Dorothy "Dee" Read of Hertford, North Carolina, owner of the Nixon Cottage, one of the original thirteen. Read is a great-great granddaughter of Francis Nixon. "Through the years, it's been added to many times. This was not like we lived in town. At Nags Head, we kept cows and pigs in the yard to keep the vegetation down. There were no doctors, no medicines, no communication in the beginning. My grandmother got diphtheria, and they brought the doctor in, and he spent a week.

"There were a lot of storms. One time, lightning came through the house and killed the dog.

"I never put on a pair of shoes all summer. It was a wonderful way to grow up. We'd take a crab net and a bucket and be gone half a day. I kept putting on dry bathing suits over and over. My mother used to say we came to the beach to wear out our old clothes.

"This old cottage is one of the few things I have left in my life that hasn't changed. I watched my granddaughter sweep sand off the porch the other day, and she swept it into the very same hole I used when I was her age."

Just beyond shouting distance of each other and some three hundred feet from the shoreline, the shacks stood erect on the flat beachfront, their front porches capturing sea breezes beneath their slanted roofs.

The rustic buildings did not at all resemble the fine plantation homes these vacationers lived in the rest of the year. Because wind constantly battered the Outer Banks, the rickety structures were repaired, enlarged, and improved with each passing storm and year. As families expanded, rooms were added, many along the back side, forming an **L** shape

NEED OFTEN LED TO INNOVATION, AS ON THIS DOOR
HANDLE MADE FROM AN OLD WOODEN SPOOL. IT IS
FOUND IN THE WINSTON-WALES COTTAGE.

Photo by Drew Crawford Wilson

NAGS HEAD, N. C.

LEFT: THE OLD BATHHOUSE, C. 1870, WAS MOVED IN 1935 AND DISMANTLED IN 1938.

BELOW: EXCURSION BOAT AT SOUND SIDE

Photos courtesy of Fred L. Fearing
Reproduced by Drew Crawford Wilson

THE NAGS HEAD PAVILION, ON THE SOUND SIDE, AROUND 1915

Photo courtesy of Fred L. Fearing
Reproduced by Drew Crawford Wilson

to shelter porch sitters from angry northeast winds.

Each cottage has its own unique history. One was built near the sound and moved to the ocean when construction began there. Another was prefabricated in Bertie County and shipped by steamer down the Roanoke River through the shallow Albemarle Sound to Nags Head, where it was assembled next to the ocean. Others were lost to northeasters and hurricanes, their families rebuilding, repairing, remodeling around original walls, even salvaging pieces to fashion new cottages altogether. Fire destroyed at least one.

Possum Silver's legacy, the Winston-Wales Cottage, built around 1875 and long thought to be the second one on the beach, is a typical Nags Head structure. Though a new section was added a few years

ago, the original part of the house has no air conditioning or heat, no full bath. Floors creak with each step. The narrow wooden stairs leading to the small upstairs rooms are original to the house, well worn from five generations of beach-drenched feet. Silver's great-grandfather Duncan Winston bought the house in 1883. His mother, Betty Wales Silver Howison of Raleigh, was a child growing up in Edenton when she and her family traveled by boat across the Albemarle Sound to Nags Head to spend the summer in what she calls her "three-century house."

"When I was a child, I remember meeting the steamer *Trenton* at the wharf in Elizabeth City. We rode across the sound, and the servants met us at the wharf. There was a cart on rails, and they pushed the luggage up the pier on a cart pulled by a horse.

The first thing I did was run to see if the ocean was still there, and it was. I learned to swim in that ocean. . . . They taught us not to be afraid of it the first three years of our lives, and to be afraid of it the rest."

Although the Nags Head area includes South Nags Head, Whalebone Junction, and Nags Head to the south, Kill Devil Hills, Kitty Hawk, Duck, and points north, Howison's cottage sits in what is now the most secluded part. Newcomers vacationing in houses shut tight against the breeze miss the charm, she says, that comes from staying where you can see sand through the cracks in the floor. Howison has spent much of

CLIMBING JOCKEY'S RIDGE, AN AGELESS PASTIME, C. 1900
Courtesy of the Outer Banks History Center

her life here, growing up with the children in adjacent houses, who are now her oldest friends.

"We used to take house parties down there," she says, "six or eight girls at a time. I remember one time when we all got sunburned. The servant patted me all over the back with cold mashed potatoes to take the heat out. Her name was Munh—you can't spell it. She lived in the backyard, couldn't read or write. She smoked a pipe and cigars, and waddled, she was so plump."

In the summer of 1904, Nags Headers explored to the north, combing the flats around the large sand dunes south of Kitty Hawk, some five miles away. The winter before, Orville and Wilbur Wright had made their historic first flight there, and stories of pieces of the plane brought natives and summer residents to comb the area for souvenirs.

"One of the Wright brothers' flights failed, an experimental flight," says Dee Read of the story she always heard. "The residents had found a lot of broken pieces through the years and kept them as souvenirs. When they tried to reconstruct [their airplane], the Wright brothers asked everybody to send them what they had. They sent my grandmother a piece of it encased in plastic, with a letter of gratitude."

Though most of the cottages were built for families in nearby mainland towns, one family traveled from faraway Charlotte. The Dranes, a second-generation Nags Head family by the early twentieth century, rode the train across the state to Elizabeth City to catch the *Trenton*. Jaquelin Drane Nash is the grand-daughter of the Reverend Dr. Robert Brent Drane, rector of St. Paul's Episcopal Church in Edenton from 1876 to 1932, who spent the warm months in Nags Head tending his summering flock. Nash's father grew up in Edenton and summered in Nags Head, and though he later moved to Charlotte, he was determined to baptize his family in the Nags Head tradition.

"I made my first trip to the beach in 1912, to my grandfather's place, when I was two years old," Mrs. Nash recalls. "We would ride the train to Elizabeth City, and we had to rush from the train station to the dock. We could hear the *Trenton*'s whistle blowing. We always worried, would the boat leave us? It seemed as though we had the same captain, who was the driver all my life. I wanted to make a table of the wheel when the *Trenton* was broken up, but at the time, I didn't have fifty dollars to my name. Now, I wish I could have borrowed it.

"When we got to the dock, my mother would take off our shoes and stockings. Jordan Peterson always came to get us with his Banker pony and a cart with high wheels. I remember the ladies would climb

A VIEW FROM THE PORCH
MANY A NAGS HEAD HOUR HAS BEEN SPENT RELAXING ON A PROTRUDING BENCH WITH A VIEW OF THE OCEAN.

Photo by Drew Crawford Wilson

PICTURED HERE IS AN OLD-FASHIONED DOOR PULL MADE OF ROPE. THIS DOOR PULL HANGS ON THE WINSTON-WALES COTTAGE, ONE OF THE THIRTEEN ORIGINAL COTTAGES AT NAGS HEAD, WHICH WAS BUILT AROUND 1875.
Photo by Drew Crawford Wilson

up on their trunks in their long dresses and ride over to the beach. But we would run at top speed, up and down the sand hills, until we could see the ocean and the cottage. We could see the marshland and the grass, and Grandmother and Aunt Nannie at the top of the steps. It was a wonderful moment. We didn't waste much time greeting the elders. We would run right to the ocean."

On weekdays in Nags Head in those early years,

children roamed barefoot through the dunes from dawn until dusk, fishing in the ponds near Nags Head Woods—a rare maritime forest of live oaks—and crabbing on the edge of the sound. They listened to tales spun by grandparents as night descended and sand fiddlers wandered out of hiding to dance in the shadows.

On Friday afternoons, the children waited eagerly for the boats that brought their fathers from town to spend the weekends with their families.

"My father was always interested in the stars," says Jaquelin Nash. "He mapped the heavens above Nags Head on deep blue engineer's paper. I can remember lying on the beach, our feet toward the ocean, learning the constellations in the northeast quadrant. We never looked in the western sky."

Sundays were different. Sundays meant church for every Nags Header.

Though Virginia Dare was christened on Roanoke Island, little is known about the presence of the Anglican Church on the Outer Banks until the nineteenth century, when parishioners from Edenton and Elizabeth City decided to build a summer church. In 1849, a small chapel named All Saints' was built on the sound side. On August 18, 1850, the sanctuary was consecrated on the anniversary of Virginia Dare's birth.

During the Civil War, the church was dismantled by Union troops, its wood used to build a refuge for runaway slaves on nearby Roanoke Island. Yet the cottagers continued their weekly worship. For fifty summers thereafter, they met each Sunday morning at the Nags Head Hotel or on cottage porches.

Early in the twentieth century, church leaders sought restitution from Congress for the dismantled building, collecting around seven hundred dollars toward building a new church. Dr. Drane, the summer rector, was put in charge of hiring someone to build the church. In 1915, he turned to a wiry Elizabeth City carpenter by the name of Stephen J. Twine, who had recently begun building new structures along the beachfront.

The original contract between the church and Twine, set down in Drane's handwriting, laid forth the specifications of the new church. The building was to be twenty-five feet wide and fifty feet long and have five windows on each long side. Two windows were to be on the west and one large window on the east. "The price agreed upon for this work shall be three hundred and twenty-seven and one-half dollars payable . . . in three installments," the document read. It was signed on August 16, 1915, by Dr. Drane and Twine.

St. Andrew's-by-the-Sea was built near the site of the original church, between low dunes near the Roanoke Sound. It soon became a center of life at Nags Head. Children walked barefoot to Sunday school and slapped mosquitoes from their legs while listening to stories of Moses and Noah.

"We went to church whenever there was a minister there," Betty Howison recalls. "The mosquitoes

THE FOREMAN-HARRIS COTTAGE, ORIGINALLY CALLED THE CLAY FOREMAN COTTAGE, IS IN THE FOREGROUND AS YOU LOOK SOUTH ALONG THE NAGS HEAD BEACHFRONT. BUILT BY S. J. TWINE IN 1910, THIS WAS HIS FIRST OCEANFRONT DESIGN.

Courtesy of the
Outer Banks History Center

nearly ate us alive. They tried to put the church between two dunes, and the water was standing underneath it all the time."

"St. Andrew's played a big part in our lives," says Tom Skinner of Elizabeth City, another descendant of Francis Nixon. "We grew up summering at Nags Head during the 1930s. Most of us were Episcopalian. When I was a boy, we'd go underneath the church and sail handmade boats in the puddles if the sermons ran too long."

The sea's influence on St. Andrew's was constant.

Legend says that Dr. Drane had been praying for a door for the new church when one washed ashore that fit the hole just right.

"It's an old Nags Head story that makes a little bit light of a very devout man," says Jaquelin Nash of her grandfather. "He probably did pray for a door. People don't think of how terribly poor the life was out there, both for the Bankers and the rest, how far away you were from everything. You made do with what you had."

THIS IS THE CLAY FOREMAN COTTAGE, ALSO KNOWN AS THE FOREMAN-HARRIS COTTAGE, AS IT LOOKS TODAY. WHERE ONCE THERE WAS A FLAT BEACH, DUNES WITH SEA OATS STAND GUARD AGAINST THE BREAKERS.
Photo by Drew Crawford Wilson

The Patron Saint
The Reverend Dr. Robert Brent Drane

REVEREND DR. ROBERT BRENT DRANE, RECTOR OF ST. ANDREW'S-BY-THE-SEA, AND HIS
GRANDCHILDREN—ELIZABETH WEBB, MARIA DRANE, JOE WEBB, JAQUELIN DRANE, AND BOB DRANE—RELAX
ON THE BEACH AROUND 1921. THE DUNSTAN-DRANE COTTAGE STANDS IN THE BACKGROUND.
Courtesy of Florence Nash

Men were not a weekday fixture at the Nags Head cottages during the summer, except for the Reverend Dr. Robert Brent Drane, who followed his Edenton congregation to the beach. There, in a cottage he shared with his wife and sister-in-law, Drane greeted the grandchildren who came to spend the summer weeks. Jaquelin Nash, one of those grandchildren, came every August, the first time in 1912, when she was two years old.

When the grandchildren arrived, the Dranes would line them up and review the house rules, penciled on a list and nailed to the door of their cottage, eye-level to a child: Don't talk about disgusting things at the table; never leave the house without telling a grownup; hang up your bathing suit or you can't go swimming; everyone must be silent for one hour after lunch.

Jaquelin Nash remembers well those summer days

ST. ANDREW'S-BY-THE-SEA EPISCOPAL CHURCH, C. 1917
Courtesy of the Outer Banks History Center

spent with her grandfather, including how, even on the hottest of days, he would wear his black suit and clerical collar.

Grandfather had gone from Edenton on a sailboat and took a fisherman's hut because he had to have a place to spend the night. There was a porch that ran the back length of the cottage, and they enclosed it to make a dining room, but they left a window that came down almost to the floor. We children loved to crawl through that window; we never used the door.

They said he enlarged the cottage—and the sailboat, named the Skip Jack—every time he had another child, and he had seven children. They said every time my grandmother had a baby, he would saw the boat in half and add a new section. But I always thought that was just a story.

He always wore his clerical collar at the beach, and

when we woke up, he would give thanks for the new day. Every morning and every evening, Grandfather had family prayers. Everybody in the cottage would gather together and sit quietly, and the servants would come in from the kitchen—we had three servants—and sit with the family, and we'd have prayers. The children vied for the window sill. . . . We'd see how many of us we could fit in the window as Grandfather said his prayers.

They were the most beautiful old prayers that got stuck in my mind. In the morning, he always gave thanksgiving for the new day, and he always prayed for safety at night. I grew up realizing that danger at night was a very real thing in the minds of old people.

He was the patron saint of Roanoke Island. Every year, he'd take his nimble grandchildren in the sailboat to Manteo to gather figs. And in August, we always went to Fort Raleigh, to the place he knew Virginia Dare had been baptized, and one island baby would be baptized with the name Virginia Dare. We would be acolytes, altar guild, sponsor—whatever he needed us to be.

After the rainy season, the church would be surrounded by little ponds full of tiny green frogs. I remember how it felt to sit by the open window, to be part of the whole thing. I will never forget that smell—the hot wood, lattice and salt water, heavy together.

St. Andrew's was so much my grandfather's church. There were no clocks, but they rang a bell that told you when it was time to go to church. (Years later, when they renovated the church, nobody had hung the bell in

COUSINS GATHER ON THE PORCH OF THE DUNSTAN-DRANE COTTAGE. FROM LEFT, KATHERINE DRANE, BRENT DRANE, FLORENCE DRANE, MARIAN DRANE, MARIA DRANE, ROBERT B. DRANE, ROBERT DRANE JR., JAQUELIN DRANE, BOB DRANE.
Courtesy of Florence Nash

the belfry, so I got some boys to help me, and I climbed up myself.)

I remember the sand embedded in the walls, because it had blown so hard during a hurricane.

The only time we wore shoes was when we went to church. Both my sister and I were organists. . . . There was always somebody in the Drane family at the organ, generation by generation.

My grandfather taught me to swim. He spent a lot of time with the children in the water. I remember he had a long, gray beard, and he took me out over my head. We were doing so well, until an unexpected roller came along and knocked me out of his arms. I remember flailing around, desperate to find his beard.

We had rules about taking a midday nap, no scuffling on the bed. He was very stern, but we knew he loved us.

We used to love to sing camp songs on the beach at night. We'd sit near the edge of the ocean. My cousins and my siblings and I had some pretty good voices, and I remember once, we were out on the beach singing "Holy, Holy, Holy" in four parts, and Grandfather came down, knelt down on his knees, and prayed. It was so touching, so moving. We were always very reverent about our singing.

Our cottage was next door to the Arlington Hotel. We'd hear the band being set up on Sunday afternoons, but we were told to go to the north porch to be away from the music. What he thought the music was going to do to us, I don't know.

PLAYING IN THE WATER IS AN AGE-OLD PASTIME AS EVIDENCED BY THE DRANE COUSINS, MARIA DRANE, JAQUELIN DRANE, BOB DRANE, ELIZABETH WEBB, ELIZABETH HANES, AND JOE WEBB, DRESSED IN THEIR BATHING COSTUMES AROUND 1920.
Courtesy of Florence Nash

JAQUELIN DRANE, ELIZABETH WEBB, BOB DRANE, JOE WEBB, AND MARIA DRANE POSE IN THEIR SUNDAY BEST ON THE DRANE PORCH AROUND 1924.
Courtesy of Florence Nash

THE DRANE COTTAGE, ONE OF THE UNPAINTED ARISTOCRACY'S ORIGINAL THIRTEEN, WAS BUILT IN 1887. IT WAS ALSO KNOWN AS THE H. V. DUNSTAN COTTAGE OR THE DUNSTAN-DRANE COTTAGE. THIS PHOTOGRAPH WAS TAKEN AROUND 1900.
Courtesy of the Outer Banks History Center

The house on the beach was a center. He would sometimes be sitting on the porch and up would come, in the old days, a Banker pony pulling a cart and some of his old friends who were the old inhabitants, who'd come across the water in their boats from Manteo. They'd sit on the porch with Grandfather and chew the rag in their broad "hoi toid" accents. They'd talk about old times on the beach—wonderful stories of shipwrecks, life-saving on the beach, and the heroism of the men who did it.

My father loved those particular times. He never missed those sessions, because things that were going to be lost forever would be talked about. We were old enough to know something marvelous was going on. You love it before you are conscious of what it is.

"The Beach was his whole life."
The Story of S. J. Twine

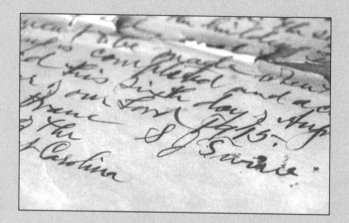

LEFT: LAURA AND S. J. TWINE ON A WALKWAY IN NAGS HEAD, C. 1910. TWINE IS RESPONSIBLE FOR THE SIGNATURE NAGS HEAD LOOK: PROTRUDING PORCH BENCHES, PROPPED SHUTTERS, AND FULL-WIDTH DORMERS. *Courtesy of Laura D. Twine*
ABOVE: THE ORIGINAL CONTRACT TO BUILD ST. ANDREW'S-BY-THE-SEA, SIGNED BY REVEREND DR. ROBERT BRENT DRANE, RECTOR, AND S. J. TWINE IN AUGUST 1915. *Photo by Susan Byrum Rountree*

The small, bespectacled man in the floppy gray hat was a fixture in Nags Head. His carpenter's box strapped over his shoulder, Elizabeth City's Stephen J. Twine—all five feet, two inches of him—made the daily walk from his string of sound-side rental shacks to the cottages he was building along the beachfront.

From the second decade of the twentieth century until the 1940s, many of the cottages—and St. Andrew's-by-the-Sea—were built by the hands of S. J. Twine. Though the true number is unknown, over a dozen of the sixty structures that now sit within the Nags Head Beach Cottage Row Historic District were built by

Twine. They are his signature, their **L** shapes blocking the northeast wind, shutters propped open just wide enough to keep the sun out and let sea breezes in.

It was Twine who was most responsible for the distinctive architectural style of the cottages of Nags Head. Working with the tools he kept in his carpenter's box—hammer, saw, plane, and a bottle filled with turpentine to keep the saw limber—Twine fashioned cottages so sturdy they would withstand a century of hurricanes and northeasters, losing barely a shingle.

Charlie Reber, a native Nags Header, lived across from Twine during the summers when he was a boy.

"Old man Twine was the first major builder to dwell in Nags Head," says Reber. "Originally, they were small, boxy camps. He built them to fit the landscape, the slope of the beach. He built the roofline so that as the wind would blow on the roof and raise up off it, it would cause pressure to push down on it, rather than lift them off. It's been told that not one of Mr. Twine's cottages has ever lost a roof or was blown apart. Halwood Culpepper [was] another builder at the time. . . . They said he could build any building for you as long as Mr. Twine approved it.

"Most of his designs were similar—strong houses, and easy houses to move. He built those cottages like a puzzle; one piece couldn't move unless the others did. This had a whole lot to do with why they were able to withstand so many storms.

"He knew how to stand the timbers, running the uprights from the first floor to the second floor—one piece of wood tying the whole house together. A lot of them didn't have interior walls. They were tied together with corner straps.

"The houses he built were faced with juniper or cypress shingles—trees that were accustomed to water, so they wouldn't rot. I've replaced a lot of shingles on these houses, but the nails gave out before the shingles did. I built a house with used shingles from these cottages, and all I did was turn them over and renail 'em."

"There were no power tools," says Twine's nephew, Mickey Twine of Elizabeth City, who as a teenager worked with his uncle. "He built everything by hand. It might take up to eighteen months, but he worked on two or three at a time. He never cut corners when building a house."

Twine was said to favor eyeballing a straight line against the horizon of the vast Atlantic over using a level. He was also a tinkerer who had to keep his giant hands busy. He would tend to the cottagers' needs, building new structures or remodeling old cottages as families expanded. And when the ocean crept too close to the front steps of a cottage, Twine was called to move it.

"He built them to be moved," says Mickey. "He used black-gum rollers that he ran under the boards of the house, and an old capsule wench. A man worked the wench round and round. He moved some big houses that way."

As a boy, Charlie Reber saw Twine and his crew move plenty of houses. "He'd roll the rollers under the houses. There would be rollers on both sides and men on

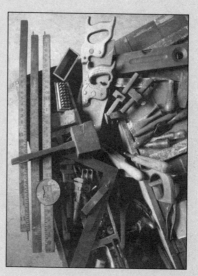

ABOVE, LEFT: S. J. TWINE STANDS IN FRONT OF THE CLAY FORE-MAN COTTAGE, WHICH WAS THE FIRST OCEANFRONT HOUSE HE BUILT AROUND 1910. *Courtesy of Laura D. Twine*

ABOVE RIGHT: WITH ONLY A FEW TOOLS THAT HE CARRIED TO AND FROM THE OCEANFRONT IN A WOODEN TOOLBOX, S. J. TWINE BUILT HOMES THAT WITHSTOOD HURRICANES AND NORTHEASTERS FOR OVER A CENTURY.

Photo by Drew Crawford Wilson

RIGHT: TWINE BUILT SEVERAL COTTAGES ON THE SOUND SIDE FOR HIMSELF AND FOR RENTERS. THE S. J. TWINE SOUND-SIDE COT-TAGE, C. 1915, IS WHERE HE SPENT HIS OFF-TIME.

Courtesy of Laura D. Twine

both sides, and they'd stick a pole in the log and would all roll at the same time. He was the first one to move some of the beach houses. He also moved houses from the sound to the ocean. He moved the hotel, of all things—all done by shovel and hand and leveling the dunes if one was in the way."

When water began surrounding St. Andrew's-by-the-Sea where it sat between the sand hills, Twine moved it to its present site, across the road from the beachfront cottages.

He was known as a calm, Christian man who rarely showed his temper. "Whenever he got tangled up," says Mickey Twine, "he'd shout, 'Thunderation!' That was his word."

Trusted both for the quality of his work and for his honesty, he was often asked to open the cottages for the owners as the weather began to warm. "At one time, he had a key to every house. He kept [them] in a bait bucket," says Mickey, who knew his uncle to clean the houses and set them up for the families. "All they had to do was walk in."

"He was always real quiet, always had glasses on," says Reber. "Twine kept a clean workplace. He was very small. They called him 'Stretch.' What he wore on Monday, he was still wearing it on Friday— a bib overall and a long-sleeved shirt. He was always toting a toolbox, and that box had about everything he needed to complete the job."

After the bridge was built over the Currituck Sound in the 1930s, Twine could often be seen riding to and from Elizabeth City in a three-wheel motorcycle driven by his friend Frank McIntyre. A two-by-six would be stretched across the back.

From March until October, Twine often stayed in Nags Head, living in a small cottage he built for himself. His adored wife, Laura, stayed behind in Elizabeth City during the week. "He treated her like she would break," says Mickey of his aunt. "He didn't want her to so much as sweep the floor.

"The beach was his whole life," says Mickey. "He didn't take a vacation. He kept his own oyster bed in the sound, and he'd go out there in the mornings and pick his oysters, and he fished a little bit, but that was all. He caught all his water in a juniper tank held up high on legs. He used it to bathe, cook with, everything. We had hominy grits and sausage for two meals a day.

"He fell off a house he was building when he was eighty-something. They had dug some sand to put the pilings in, and he fell into the sand. He didn't break a bone."

Others in his family share similar tales of his fortitude.

"When I was in junior high school," says great-nephew Clayton Twine, "I helped him build the cottage that now belongs to my sister. It took us three and a half months. It was an eight-by-twelve square box, one room with no bathroom. He bought it and added on to it—two bedrooms and a kitchen downstairs and two bedrooms upstairs. During the week, we ate a spot, a piece of white bread, and a teaspoon of mayonnaise. That was for three

LEFT: NAGS HEAD BUILDER STEPHEN J. TWINE AND WIFE LAURA POSE FOR THE CAMERA AS A YOUNG COUPLE, C. 1900. *Courtesy of Laura D. Twine*

ABOVE: S. J. AND LAURA TWINE IN NAGS HEAD, C. 1950 *Courtesy of Laura D. Twine*

CLOCKWISE FROM FRONT: KENNEDY HOUTZ,
JANE HOUTZ, LAURA TWINE, AND THE
CHILDREN'S NURSE, STANDING ON THE DOCK
BEHIND THE TWINE COTTAGE C. 1915
Courtesy of Laura D. Twine

meals a day. He was ninety-five years old by then. He laid the whole design out on a pad, the length and width of it; it all came from his head. The roof was sharp-pitched, tin. We were on the roof working right in the sun. . . . It would have killed some young boy today."

It is Twine's timeless design—the single, full-width dormers, the propped shutters, the protruding porch benches, the sloping roofs—that says *Nags Head* to passersby even today.

Low Tide

Nina Burke, Joe Webb, and Marian Drane wade in the Atlantic in August 1929.

Courtesy of Frances Drane Inglis

II. LOW-TIDE: THE BEACH-DRENCHED LIFE, 1916-1949

BEFORE THE DAYS of the water slides and minia-ture golf courses that now dot U.S. 158 Bypass be-tween Nags Head and Kitty Hawk, a child's only en-tertainments were ocean and sand. Nobody needed more. Mothers made "floats" from cotton sheets, teaching their children to race down the beach and fill them with air, then jump into the surf and float. Children of all ages roamed the dunes from the surf to the sound. They swung on natural vines in Nags Head Woods, falling into freshwater pools. On Sun-day afternoons, girls and boys danced barefoot in a pavilion by the ocean. Brave boys captured first kisses on the top of Jockey's Ridge late at night.

But the summer Nags Headers were not immune to the worries that threatened the outside world.

"I had my birthday down there every year," Jaquelin Nash remembers. "It came around in mid-August, and we planned to celebrate with a marsh-mallow roast on the beach. There were no telephones, no roads, no communication of any sort except to put your foot in the sand and walk to where you wanted to go to deliver a message. The way you in-vited people, you'd knock on the floor of the porch and ask them about the birthday party. My cousin and I had the same birthday. I remember one year, around my eighth or tenth birthday, I invited them all. We lit the fire, but nobody came. And time went on, and nobody came. I remember that as well as I remember anything in my life. It was such agony. What happened? Didn't they like me anymore? But word of polio had gotten around and gone up and down the beach. No mother would let any child leave the cottage. Why somebody didn't come and tell me, I'll never know."

By the late 1920s, Nags Head's oceanfront community was growing. S. J. Twine had added close to a dozen new cottages to the beachfront row and remodeled many of the original structures to hold new generations of families. Twine moved any cottage threatened by the ocean's breakers. He modified the roofs of others, adding new, full-width dormers of his own design, one element that would come to define Nags Head's signature cottage architecture.

The houses themselves provided adventure for the growing numbers of Nags Head children. From the upstairs rooms, they spied on adults through holes in the floor, listening in on the conversations that filtered through the wooden boards. They played under the cottages when it rained and took lazy naps on corner hammocks every afternoon when the sun blazed or the water churned too violently for swimming.

But change was coming to the isolated strip of sand. In 1928, a bridge over the Roanoke Sound opened, connecting Nags Head with Manteo. A year later, the first pilings were laid for a new bridge over the Currituck Sound to the north. Built with private money from Elizabeth City, the wooden bridge opened in the spring of 1930, connecting the north beach at Kitty Hawk with the mainland. Folks who contributed money to the project drove sixty miles

from Elizabeth City—part of the way on an unpaved road—to cross the bridge.

Elizabeth City native Fred Fearing, a self-described pack rat who has spent his life collecting the history of Nags Head in photographs, remembers the day well.

"It was a Sunday—I think April first—and I rode down there with my buddies to ride across and see Bill Jones, the man who built the bridge. We drove across, to the crest of Pryor Hill to take a look at the ocean; you thought you were driving on water. Then we turned around and came back. There were so many that day who went across to look at the ocean and turned around. You couldn't find three people up there on the beach back then. It was a long, desolate twelve miles to the Unpainted Aristocracy."

Navigating the sand road was often tricky. Drivers had to deflate their tires and keep a shovel and a plank in the car, should they get stuck. The best route was to drive across the flats to the ocean and ride down the beach at low tide.

A year later, workers completed a new paved road connecting Kitty Hawk to Nags Head, allowing cottagers to drive directly to their summer homes for the first time. Bridges on either end of the barrier island meant that anyone with an automobile could drive to Nags Head now, giving a different kind of tourist access to what had always been an exclusive beach.

In Nags Head, some locals ran thriving small businesses from their sound-side community, catering to

THIS PHOTOGRAPH OF THE COTTAGES OF THE UNPAINTED ARISTOCRACY, MOST LIKELY TAKEN IN THE EARLY 1920S, SERVES AS A REMINDER OF THE WAY THINGS USED TO BE. THE PRUDEN-BATTLE-CLARK COTTAGE STANDS TO THE FAR LEFT, AND THE WOOD-FOREMAN COTTAGE IS NEXT TO IT.

Photo courtesy of Fred L. Fearing / Reproduced by Drew Crawford Wilson

cottagers who spent most of their time on the beach. The locals provided daily rations of ice, crabs, fish, clean laundry, and fresh vegetables to the summer residents. They were fiercely independent people who gleaned their life from the sea and did not often mix with the summer residents outside of business. Most lived near the sound in shacks sheltered by wax myrtles and oaks, just as their families had done before Nags Head was discovered by the tourists. They did not encourage familiarity. Even so, Nags Head's summer residents were very dependent upon them.

Unstable weather was—and is—as much a part of the Nags Head experience as salt and sand. Hurri-

canes in 1899 and 1933 brought high winds and rain, the ocean waters washing over the dunes clear to the sound and back again. In those days, there was no road and little vegetation to break a storm's path, so the area was usually able to recover from the damage. The only warning that a storm was coming was a horse and cart manned by Coast Guard workers, who traveled the beach urging cottagers to evacuate. Often, those warnings came too late for families to make it to safer ground. Many older Nags Headers remember well the storm of August 23, 1933, when whole families had to face a hurricane inside the beachfront shacks.

Betty Howison was a child sitting on the back porch of her great-grandfather's beach cottage, feeling the sea foam blow into her face. "There was an eerie pink sunset," she recalls, "and the ocean was crashing up into the floor of the porch."

That afternoon, the Coast Guard drove a horse and cart up and down the beach, warning residents of the approaching storm.

Dee Read, Howison's neighbor, was five years old at the time. "My father drove down here to get us, but the water was too high for us to get out." The family gathered up the chickens from under the house as water sloshed across the porch. "We kept the chickens in the kitchen," says Read, "and I remember watching water seep into the walls. My grandmother said it felt like we were in the middle of the ocean on a cheap ship. After it was over, mosquitoes set up shop on the screens of the houses. You couldn't see out the windows, there were so many."

Following the heavy damage from the hurricane of 1933, many of the cottages were moved back from the ocean for the first time. The beach road broke into pieces during the storm. WPA road crews picked up the remnants and moved them over to Soundside Road, which ran from the ocean to the settlement there. They assembled the pieces into a pattern that resembled a puzzle. From then on, it was nicknamed "Jigsaw Road."

The Midgetts, one of the oldest families on the island, owned a store near the sound for years. Soon after the hurricane blew through the beach, they moved their store to the beach road across from Cottage Row. Since it was now just across the street, the store was easily accessible to the children, who would forgo their beach adventures just long enough to grab a Coca-Cola from the iced bin out front at Midgett's.

By 1934, still more changes signaled an end to the simple life in Nags Head. The next few years were marked by a transition from old to new. Electric lights, new roads, increasing numbers of tourists—all slowly nibbled away at the Nags Head tradition.

The dune called Jockey's Ridge has towered more than one hundred feet over Nags Head for centuries, drawing visitors to its unmatched vista of the entire beach. In the early years, Nags Head's summer children roamed Jockey's Ridge freely, since there was no road between their homes and the giant dune. The

FRANCES DRANE, LEFT, AND BETTY FOREMAN PLAY IN THE SAND IN 1936.
Courtesy of Frances Drane Inglis

THE DUNES OF JOCKEY'S RIDGE HAVE LONG WATCHED OVER THE COTTAGES OF THE UNPAINTED ARISTOCRACY. THOUGH NO DATE IS GIVEN, THIS PHOTOGRAPH WAS PROBABLY TAKEN AROUND 1940.

Courtesy of the North Carolina Collection, University of North Carolina Library at Chapel Hill

CLIMBING JOCKEY'S RIDGE AROUND 1939 ARE
(LEFT TO RIGHT) REBECCA DRANE, HENRIETTA COLLINS,
FRANCES DRANE, AND BETTY FOREMAN.

Courtesy of Frances Drane Inglis

summer children thought they owned the dune and sometimes used their wits to thwart efforts to change their favorite haunt.

Tom Skinner remembers well one summer in the 1930s when he and his friends sabotaged the work of the Civilian Conservation Corps, which was working to keep sand from shifting from "the Ridge."

"We used to roast hot dogs on the top of Jockey's Ridge whenever it was somebody's birthday," Skinner recalls. "A crowd of fifteen would soon grow to a hundred. We'd melt marshmallows on top of saltine crackers. In the mid-1930s, the Civilian Conservation Corps planted grass on Jockey's Ridge to keep the sand from shifting. Don't tell anybody, but there

was a group of kids who for twelve nights straight pulled every single blade up."

Summer at the beach meant swimming, which meant learning *how* to swim in the Atlantic, an often-angry ocean made dangerous by changing currents. Early-morning family swims were a tradition. When the mosquitoes were biting, children often shared the shoreline with cows that used their tails to swat the pesky insects off their backsides.

Frank Dinwiddie, the Baptist minister, was an accomplished ocean swimmer who trained Nags Head's children how to swim toward the bottom and let the sea wash over them. He also taught them how to recognize a riptide. When they recited Bible verses from memory, Dinwiddie awarded them silver fish charms. Every child worked hard to earn enough for a necklace full of fish.

But the reality of living on the beach meant that the families had to take the ocean's dangers with its joys. The children of the 1930s grew up hearing tales of near-drownings in the changing sea. Who could forget the story of Cousin Kate Nixon, who drowned one day in a riptide?

"Everybody loved Kate," says Dee Read. "Kate was in her twenties; my mother, Kate's cousin, was a girl then; she said she would never forget watching Kate's red swim cap bob in the water, getting smaller and smaller. Then, suddenly, she didn't come back up."

Bystanders called for the help of their strongest swimmer, a black servant, who tied a rope around his waist and swam out to Kate. Legend contends that the servant, afraid of wrapping his arms around a white girl for fear of what might happen to him, dragged her by the arm instead of lifting her head out of the waves.

"They used to take horses down there," Read says. "Somebody got a horse and tore up the beach, driving it to the lifesaving station to get help, which was about five miles away. They said that horse was never the same."

By the time the servant dragged Kate and himself

SALLY WOOD DIXON, BETSY WOOD, AND REBECCA DRANE POSE IN A DORY BOAT ON THE BEACH IN 1937.
Courtesy of Frances Drane Inglis

ON THE BEACH AT NAGS HEAD, C. 1920
Courtesy of the Outer Banks History Center

out of the breakers, Kate was dead. The servant crawled to shore, shaking uncontrollably. Someone handed him a bottle of liquor. Eyewitnesses claimed that he drank the whole bottle without stopping.

"They said she didn't die of drowning, that it was her heart," says Read. "The only way they could get her body off the island was by boat. So she lay in the cottage overnight. It was horrible."

⤫

Despite the concerns the weather and tragedies like the death of Kate Nixon caused parents, the children of Nags Head lived a fairly unstructured life, roaming freely all over the island even as more tourists began to trickle in.

"One time, we took off to the Coast Guard station," says Carmen Gray, a native Nags Header whose grandmother, Mattie Midgett, operated Midgett's Store. "I was about seven years old, and we didn't tell anybody where we were going. There was a northeaster brewing, and my uncle Jethro drove up and down the beach looking for us. He finally found us three miles away. The Coast Guard folks had invited us in for hot biscuits. We didn't want to go home."

It was no easier to keep track of the children in the water. Sometimes, young men in the family were drafted as lifeguards. Some families even resorted to giving their children a certain color bathing cap.

Mary Frances Buchanan Flowers, one of five Buchanan sisters from Durham who grew up in the largest of Nags Head's cottages, remembers how her family solved the problem. "There were five of us

girls, and sometimes our friends would come with us. My cousin was the lifeguard for our stretch of beach. We all wore the same color bathing cap—red—so he could keep count of five red caps bobbing in the water. Mother never went in further than her knees. But she took the water and swished it all over, and she got a good bath before it was all over. She never knew how to swim."

Mary Frances was a relative newcomer to Nags Head, making her first trip when she was twelve years old to spend the summer in the T. S. White Cottage, owned by her mother's aunt, Mattie Toms White of Hertford. Before that, the Buchanan sisters had vacationed in Wrightsville Beach with their mother and their father, John Adams Buchanan, a Durham insurance-company executive.

On their first trip to Nags Head, the Buchanan girls slept in beds with corn-shuck mattresses. "I remember when it rained," Mary Frances says. "We had to hold an umbrella up over the bed to keep the water off."

Mrs. Buchanan, who grew up in Hertford, had been raised on the Nags Head beach. It wasn't long before the family began planning a Nags Head cottage of its own.

In 1936, Mrs. Buchanan acquired a lot owned by the Whedbee family, who moved the Whedbee Cottage across the street. The Buchanans contracted with S. J. Twine to build a nine-bedroom house—what would be the largest in Nags Head—on the site. Because the Buchanans were a family of some means, their cottage would be more formal than the others among the Unpainted Aristocracy, though similar in architecture and style. Nothing so fancy as the Buchanan Cottage, its slanted shutters painted green and white, had yet been built on the beach. It boasted four bathrooms and enclosed showers off the side porch. Though the interior walls of many of Nags Head's cottages had remained unfinished through the years, Twine paneled the Buchanans' walls with beaded juniper.

The Buchanans moved into the house in the summer of 1936, bringing with them a driver for Mr. Buchanan, a nurse, a cook, and a maid, all of whom dressed in crisp uniforms every summer day.

∽

Soon after Twine put the finishing touches on the Buchanan Cottage, Nags Head began its most exciting era in recent memory.

Paul Green's outdoor drama, *The Lost Colony*—the tale of the English settlers who disappeared without a trace—had only recently begun production on Roanoke Island when First Lady Eleanor Roosevelt sat among the audience. According to locals, Mrs. Roosevelt convinced her husband to attend a performance. However, news reports credited United States representative Lindsey Warren with bringing Roosevelt to the area in time for the celebration of Virginia Dare's 350th birthday.

So, on August 18, 1937, natives and vacationers alike formed a flotilla in the Roanoke Sound to greet the thirty-first president of the United States, Franklin D. Roosevelt, who arrived on a 143-foot Coast Guard patrol boat to attend the outdoor drama. According to news reports, six yachts led the cutter from Elizabeth City down the Pasquotank River and across the Albemarle Sound into the docks at Manteo, where two hundred troops, sixty members of the North Carolina Highway Patrol, and a squad of Secret Service men managed the crowd that had gathered to greet him.

The *Elizabeth City Advance* of August 19 described the scene: "The white of their hulls and mahogany of their decking, mingling with the colorfulness of flags hung on streamers from their masts, dozens of yachts made the day here gay to greet the Coast Guard cutter bearing Roosevelt and his official party. Clicking cameras could be heard on all sides, as picture-taking fiends found a paradise of colorful scenes within their viewfinders."

"I can see him in his Panama hat," recalls Jaquelin Nash, who was a young mother by then. "Our boat sloop was decorated with my children's scarves, tied like pennants from one side to the other. I remember his secretary stood behind him, and when he saw us, he waved his hat."

Once he docked in Manteo, Roosevelt, dressed in a light Palm Beach suit, gave a brief speech at Fort Raleigh before some fifteen thousand people. After that, the president rode over the causeway to Nags Head in his open Packard convertible. He was accompanied by a motorcade carrying dozens of dignitaries, including North Carolina governor Clyde

Hoey, former governor J. C. B. Ehringhaus, and *Raleigh News and Observer* editor Jonathan Daniels.

Banners hoisted along the Roanoke Island bridge waved in the beach breeze as Roosevelt rode into Nags Head, where the Buchanans had been asked to host him for lunch. Marines stood guard in every yard surrounding the Buchanan Cottage. Secret Service agents lined both sides of the cottage from the road to the water. No pictures were allowed at the beach, and no local cottagers were invited to lunch. The Buchanan family's five servants—starched and pressed, as they were every other day at the beach—stood on the porch, waiting to meet the president.

Tom Skinner and a dozen other children watched from next door as the president walked, with the help of bodyguards, up a new ramp built a few weeks earlier at the Buchanans'.

"All the children lined up on the porch within twenty feet of President Roosevelt's car," Skinner recalls. "We didn't know then that he couldn't walk. They carried a chair inside the house for him to sit in, and then he walked, bracing himself up the ramp. He waved to all the kids. I will never forget it. The women all stood in line to sit in the chair. My grandmother sat in it before and after his visit."

It was that same year that S. J. Twine moved St. Andrew's-by-the-Sea to the beach road in front of the Unpainted Aristocracy, bringing the sanctuary closer to the cottages.

༄

The Nags Headers maintained their idyllic sum-

SCAFFOLDS BRACE THE SIDES AND ROOF OF St. Andrew's-by-the-Sea in this photograph that was taken when the belltower was added in 1937.

Courtesy of Florence Nash

mer lives for a few years more. Daylight meant swimming and crabbing and combing the dunes. After supper, they'd walk to the post office, located across the road from the cottages in Hollowell's Hotel. Mr. Graham Hollowell, the postmaster, had a reputation for reading postcards before handing them out to the recipients.

A few other merchants had followed the cottagers to the oceanfront in the first part of the 1930s. Mom-and-pop motor courts sprouted along the new beach road, offering efficiencies for rent to families of modest means.

In 1938, G. T. "Ras" Wescott, Jr., opened a dance hall and bowling alley called the Nags Head Casino in an old wooden building in front of Jockey's Ridge, across the road from the expanding Cottage Row. The building had been used as a barracks for the stone-cutters who built the new memorial honoring the Wright brothers' first flight at Kill Devil Hills, a few miles north of the Unpainted Aristocracy.

Though Nags Headers had been dancing in the pavilion for some time now, the Nags Head Casino would become a magnet for summer gatherings for the next forty years, not only for locals and cottagers, but for music lovers all over eastern North Carolina and Tidewater Virginia. Teenagers and older folks flocked to the Casino to practice the hottest dances of their generations—the Jitterbug, the Bop, the Twist, the Shag—on the waxed wooden floor. They danced to the music of every major big band in the country—Glen Miller, Guy Lombardo, Artie Shaw—as well as later acts like the Platters and the Carolina Ridge Runners. Louis Armstrong and Fats Domino performed to packed houses at the Casino, their music drifting out of the upstairs windows far across the dunes and through the silky summer air.

In the late 1930s and early 1940s, the Casino was the social center of the Outer Banks. On a big Saturday night at the Casino, dancers checked their shoes at the door, tossing them into a giant trough, to be retrieved after last call. The barefoot dancers packed like sardines onto the dance floor, which Wescott's workers had waxed until it glistened like glass. He

BECAUSE CASINO OWNER RAS WESCOTT DID NOT ALLOW SHOES ON THE DANCE FLOOR IN THE 1940s, DANCERS CHECKED THEIR SHOES AT THE DOOR.
Courtesy of the Outer Banks History Center

hung beach towels from the ceiling as baffles to improve the sound. The dancing literally rocked the house.

"We were there when the doors opened, and we were there to close it down," says Carmen Gray. "And we'd swear we were not going to go the next night. Then somebody would come along and ask us to go again. I was a teenager. We didn't drink or smoke, but, Lord, did we dance. I saw a lot of black musicians. On a big night, you had to pay five dollars to get in. That was Louis Armstrong. There were sixteen hundred people there that night. And that floor was moving eight inches up and down. It was just so exciting."

Wescott brought every kind of live music imaginable to his dance hall, from the fifteen-piece bands of Duke Ellington and Tommy Dorsey to, in later years, the Temptations and the Four Tops. Marquees shouting the names of upcoming bands were familiar sights posted on light poles from Hatteras to Virginia Beach. Wescott loved Hawaiian music and was known to produce a hula floor show on occasion. And whenever the bands took a break, the popular tunes of the day twirled on the Wurlitzer jukebox in the corner.

But despite the music that drifted across the street and over to the cottages each night of summer, despite all the changes that had come to Nags Head— the new road, electricity, a thriving tourist trade— the Nags Headers still lived simply, spinning stories from their front-porch rockers, listening to the roar of the ocean, and gazing up at the Milky Way spilling across the sky. Little did they know that, soon, dangerous strangers would linger within a mile of shore, watching the porch lights and the shadows of Nags Headers combing the beach.

~

As the United States entered World War II, the quiet sky Nags Headers had known for over a century exploded with noise and light. Though the war

was centered in Europe and the Pacific, Nags Headers saw and felt the conflict within sight of their front porches.

"We have gone across the beach to the ocean and seen as many as thirteen of our ships burning at one time," recalls Carmen Gray, who was a child during the war. "Our curtains had to be black or dark green, and shades had to be down before dark. There weren't many cars, but half the headlights had to be painted black. They patrolled on horseback from one lifesaving station to the next. They used to tease Peach, my grandmother, because she was scared of horses, and they'd ride them into the store."

After Pearl Harbor, the Germans set about attacking East Coast shipping lanes, though officially there was no coastal war. It would be three years before what Nags Headers saw with their own eyes was publicly verified. An eloquently written story in the *News and Observer* in June 1945 told of a battle in the early months of 1942, when some twenty-seven ships were sunk within sight of the Cape Hatteras Lighthouse, sixty miles south of Nags Head. Fantastic tales made it into print as well. The Nazis—like pirates trolling the waters more than a century earlier—reportedly lured the ship *Australia* to its doom by installing a light on the Diamond Shoals Lightship, after it had been extinguished at the beginning of the war.

"Night after night," the *News and Observer* reported, "the skies above the 'Graveyard of the Atlantic' were red with the flames of doomed and sinking ships, and day after day, the horizon was dim with smoke in a small segment of the Battle for the Atlantic in which the German submarine strove against the unprepared heroism of a Nation.

"The Germans bagged their biggest prize when the British tanker *Empire Gem* carrying 10,600 tons of gasoline literally exploded into the night with a flash that was visible for 50 miles and a roar that was heard in Elizabeth City. February came, then March, the bitterest month of the war off Hatteras, when a total of 13 merchantmen were destroyed in 18 days, and on one night nine burning ships were visible. . . . Officially there was no war off Hatteras. No communiques were ever issued about it, and no announcements of any sort were made from any quarter. Details contained within this narrative were collected from unofficial sources and are presented here because there is no longer any enemy who could be comforted by a recitative of how grim was that battle that roared above the shallows of the Outer Diamonds."

In 1945, the United States Navy released a report of the war fought off the Carolina coast: 79 ships sunk, 843 merchant seamen and gun crew lost, almost 426,000 tons of cargo lost at sea. Most of those ships were lost during the first few months of the war.

"It really goes back to World War I," says David Stick of Kitty Hawk, author of *Graveyard of the Atlantic, The Outer Banks of North Carolina*, and *The Outer Banks Reader* and a man revered by many as *the* Outer Banks historian. "Back then, Germans had submarines longer than a football field and sent them over here and sank a number of coastal ships [in the shipping lanes up and down the East Coast]. They were so successful that when World War II came along, they concentrated on building a submarine fleet, making them even larger than before. They could stay at sea for a very long time. They sent three over initially, then they sent even more. All this took place in the first four months of 1942, just after Pearl Harbor. Our defenses were not really developed until about April of that year.

"Pretty soon," says Stick, "they began to form packs just outside the shipping lanes, not more than a few miles from shore and close enough that they could see the lights from shore. There was no blackout initially. The Germans wiped out ships in great numbers, as many as seventy-five in the first four months of the war. It was a real slaughter. We didn't have any military vessels here because they'd all been sent out to guard the troops going to Europe, but they put together a patchwork fleet. There was a Civil Air Patrol base at Manteo and blimps that operated out of Elizabeth City, flying over [and] trying to spot the subs from the air. There was real concern on the Outer Banks about what was happening. They established an army camp near Kitty Hawk with a lookout tower, so they could see the ships as they approached. But the lights on shore caused a problem, and they ordered the blackout. After that time, we did sink some of the German submarines."

Despite the dangers of a coastal war, Nags Head, as always, drew the cottagers to their seaside homes.

"The Coast Guard patrolled the beach at night," Jaquelin Nash remembers. "We went down out of season and stayed in one of the oldest cottages—the Bond Cottage. And we'd go down in cool weather, because they had a fireplace. We'd crank up the wood stove to get the house warm. On balmy nights, we sat out on the porch. This was during wartime, and the beach was very carefully controlled at night, because of the submarines offshore.

"We were on the porch one night, and somebody had baked a perfectly wonderful coconut cake. The Coast Guard horse patrol came by and told us to put out the light. The man was a dear friend, and he came up and had cake, then asked me if I'd like to ride the next leg.

"It was pitch black on that horse. I had on a belt with a .45 [pistol] and a walkie-talkie. There was not a chink of light.

"My uncle, Reverend Fred Drane, was a wonderful photographer. During the war, he climbed up on Jockey's Ridge with his camera equipment. He wanted to get panoramic pictures. Up rolled a Jeep, roaring up the sand hill. The young driver thought Uncle Fred was a spy. He said, 'I'm Fred Drane. I've been coming here all my life.' They took him down, wondering who could vouch for him. He called the name of one of the old reprobates, one of his fishing buddies. 'Find old so-and-so. He'll tell you who I am.' They found old so-and-so, who said, 'That's Fred Drane.

I've known him all my life.' "

Rationing was in place in Nags Head, just like everywhere else during the war.

"Everybody paid with ration cards during the war," says Carmen Gray. "People would get so mad at my grandmother. She would order fifteen pounds of butter and wouldn't get but ten. The ladies who baked a lot of cakes would get so mad because they wanted their butter. They had the ration coupons for it. But she made sure everybody got a little bit. The same thing with sugar and gas."

By the summer of 1942, the unofficial coastal war was raging. Curfews and blackout curtains came with it. No one was allowed to drive at night with full headlights. A Civil Air Patrol station was based on Roanoke Island, and the navy began construction of a lighter-than-air station in Weeksville, near Elizabeth City.

Jockey's Ridge, the favored spot for marshmallow roasts, soon became littered with bombs. Reports that the huge sand hill was a target for bombers stationed near Manteo remained officially unsubstantiated, though locals still believe this to be true.

"They say there was a bombing range up at Duck, but that was later," says Carmen Gray. "There was no range there during World War II. It was at Jockey's Ridge. They would tell us the hours they were going to use it, to keep us out of the yard, keep us off the Ridge. Somehow, we knew. I've got bombs that landed in my backyard. We would chase those dirigibles; we just knew we could catch one. The mooring cable

Spider Villa (right), built by W. W. Griffin in 1859, was one of Nags Head's original thirteen. It became the beachfront home of Reverend Fred B. Drane in 1936. It is now known as the Warren-Miles-Hoffman Cottage. The Winston-Wales cottage stands in the background of this photograph.

Courtesy of Francis Drane Inglis

(From left to right) Reverend Henry Johnson, Virginia Drane, Marian Drane Graham with Frances Drane, and Dr. Frank Porter Graham gather at the beach in 1936. Cottage Row stands in the background.

Courtesy of Frances Drane Inglis

would be hanging down. Usually, they were bringing supplies to the Outer Banks."

Carmen Gray remembers how the war provided a lifelong reminder for one member of her family. "There were eight of us, up there on Jockey's Ridge during the war, and my brother picked up a hand grenade fuse and pulled the pin. It blew three fingers of his right hand off. He was eleven years old. The hand grenade fuses washed up by the case on the beach, and the service-station men played with them, and they'd throw them out back. It was not placed there by anybody, just somehow got there."

Mothers now patrolled the beach in the mornings before allowing their children to swim and play freely. Every now and then, they'd spy an object bobbing in the breakers and call all the children inside, only to discover it was a swimmer, not a body washing ashore.

The Casino became a gathering place for sailors on leave. Many a night, the sailors would pick fights with locals and with each other, tossing their hats out the windows into piles in the parking lot. Sporadically, someone would call the crowd outside to watch as a ship burned at sea.

On Wednesdays, organized fights became the draw. Ras Wescott and his crew hoisted a full-size boxing ring in through the upstairs windows. Patrons from the surrounding communities would flock to the Casino to watch men from Manteo and elsewhere fight it out inside the ring.

The locals, entrenched in their century-old habit of combing the beach for their livelihood, searched for remnants of ships. K rations bobbed in the water, and it wasn't unusual to find cigarettes, malted milk candy, and even raisin bread among the boxes that drifted to shore.

Native Nags Header Charlie Reber remembers finding an eight-foot torpedo and a life raft large enough to carry twenty people. Once, a parachute washed ashore. His mother made it into curtains and a sail for his wagon. "Just to tell you how few people were on the beach, that life raft had K rations in compartments, and for a long time—probably a year or more—you could go to that life raft and get rations out of it. Today, if you'd leave a boat or a car on the beach overnight, you'd lose your motor or prop or gas tank.

"When ships would go by," says Reber, "they'd throw overboard everything they didn't use. We hardly ever had to buy a light bulb. We'd hold them up to see if they had water in them. Apples—the salt made them taste good—bananas by the bunch, pineapples and oranges, even coconuts. I was about ten years old, and Mom gave us a little kitchen hammer, and we beat the coconut and loosened the meat from the shell."

During the summer months, Nags Head natives, like their Banker ancestors, continued to earn their livelihoods from the cottagers, most of whom were by now leaving their cows and chickens—but not their servants—at home when they came to the beach.

"A story that never got told is about the pioneers down here," says Carmen Gray. "Ezeta Reber and Blanche Johnson took in laundry. Mrs. Reber took it to her house, and she'd wash and iron for five dollars a basket. She starched the sheets and pillowcases and the men's shirts so that they stood on the floor. Both of them cleaned cottages. When people were coming, they did the spring cleaning. They'd air everything out and get it ready for the folks to come down. And Lena Mae Reber peddled crabs on her bicycle. She put them in a basket of sea grass and sold them for five cents apiece."

The Rebers were jacks-of-all-trades. In addition to doing laundry, they provided plumbing services (Charlie Reber's grandfather was the first licensed plumber in Nags Head), painting services, and cottage cleaning and repair. As a boy, Reber earned money picking up sand spurs in the cottage yards. As S. J. Twine began to age, the cottagers called on Reber's father, Edward, who had helped Twine from time to time, to open the houses up in the spring and do minor repairs in the winter.

In time, Charlie, a lifelong tinkerer, took his place, growing to know the families well. "I've shingled every single one of those houses at least once," he says. "I had keys to every cottage. If we were fixing one of them, they'd say, 'Stay in the cottage, if you like.' Sometimes, I would stay just to listen to the ocean. The freedom these people gave us made us feel like we were part of the family. I was the electrician, painter, plumber, carpenter. The name Reber was always written somewhere on the kitchen wall.

"Come Labor Day, though, it was like pulling a curtain on a Broadway show. You could sleep on the road, and not a single car would pass."

During the cold months, the highway and the empty beach became the playground for Nags Head's winter children.

"One of our big things to do in the winter," says Carmen Gray, "was to go under the cottage line where they sat on their seats, after a northeaster, to get all the change that had fallen out of their pockets.

"We'd stand on top of those hills with sea oats on them in front of the Skinners' cottage, and we'd stand—I swear, I don't know why we didn't all die—and hold on to those sea oats, and those waves would hit that thing until it would cave in, and down we'd go. We have to run all the way to the Nixons' before the next wave would get us. I don't know why we weren't all swept to sea.

"I remember one winter [when] a cottage caught fire, and the wind was blowing, and it took three of them—one, two, three, right in a row."

Finally, the war was over, and Nags Headers once again climbed Jockey's Ridge to celebrate, roasting hot dogs and marshmallows and telling ghost stories in the firelight.

"I always wanted to see a storm at Nags Head."
The Hurricane of 1933

A WOMAN STANDS INSIDE THE BASE OF A BUILDING IN NAGS HEAD AFTER THE 1933 HURRICANE.
Photo courtesy of Fred L. Fearing / Reproduced by Drew Crawford Wilson

Virginia Flora Hall grew up in Elizabeth City and vacationed at Nags Head with her family in the James Gatlin Cottage, built in 1868 and bought by her father in the early 1900s. Born in 1900, Mrs. Hall spent many a summer night at Nags Head in the days before electricity came to the Outer Banks. But no night was as memorable as that of August 22-23, 1933, when a hurricane hit during high season. That hurricane is remembered by old-time Nags Headers for its flooding tides and torrential rains.

Mrs. Hall recalls her early days in Nags Head, and how the storm hit just after she and her husband sat down to supper.

A VIEW OF SOUND SIDE AFTER THE 1933 HURRICANE
Photo courtesy of Fred L. Fearing / Reproduced by Drew Crawford Wilson

My father died when I was twelve years old. He thought it was healthy if we went down to the beach and stayed all summer. We went down on the Hattie Creef, *and we took a horse, a cart, and a couple of chickens, and five hundred pounds of ice. When I think about that little boat, I wonder, how did they get all that on that little boat? Everybody went, and they all went on the* Hattie Creef *except the Outlaws. They had a boat.*

My father had a drink every night. And he'd give me the sugar from it. I looked forward to going on the side porch and drinking the sugar. I must have been about six or seven.

All the cottages were rugged. We had to clean the lanterns every morning. We had chamber pots in every room, and slop jars. Two outhouses, one for the men and one for the ladies. Our house was in sections. There was an open place where you had stacked wood, then there was the servants' cottage. They had a wash house out back.

During Prohibition, my husband's brother made beer in the wash house. He threw all the mash out the window. In that day and time, all the pigs and animals were roaming around, and all the pigs ate the mash and got drunk. Next door to our cottage, there was a boarding house, and everybody was out on the porch watching the pigs. They would run up against each other and punch and carry on. It was the funniest thing you've ever seen.

We met the mail every night, came home and ate supper, then walked back to the sound side to the pavilion. There were no screens, just a big dance floor. Every Sunday, we went over to . . . get a cup of ice cream. It took all day walking to the sound and back. One time, some drunk was on the boat, and Dr. Drane, with his long white beard, was standing on the dock, and the drunk said, "There's Santy Claus."

Every morning, the colored man who worked for my father would ride up to the fresh ponds. Of course, we had carts that came around and sold vegetables. Every Wednesday, they had meat in the carts, and we couldn't wait till then. I tell you, it'd be hot, and they'd have it covered with dirty old cheesecloth, and the flies would be so thick on it. We couldn't wait to eat it, and nobody ever got sick. It's all in what your system's accustomed to.

There was a lady, Mrs. Wise, who used to do laundry for five cents apiece, whether it was a sheet or a handkerchief.

When we went swimming, it was something else. We wore shoes, a dress, hat, a bathing costume made of slick black fabric. It was so heavy. During the day, we wore a skirt, never above the knees, and a middy blouse. We were mostly barefooted.

My mother never liked Nags Head. She couldn't sleep. She said she kept waiting for the next wave to

WATCHING THE WINDS OF CHANGE
THE BUCHANAN BAROMETER KEEPS TRACK
OF THE CHANGING NAGS HEAD WEATHER.
Photo by Drew Crawford Wilson

break. But she stayed.

The help always brought a pig and fed him off the scraps from the table all summer. The man said that pig lasted him all winter after it was slaughtered. We had a chicken coop on the corner of the house. One time, we had a big northeaster, and the sand blew the feathers right off the chickens. So we ate chickens for three or four days.

Back then, you knew who the strangers were.

When hurricanes came back then, they rode around

the night before. The Coast Guard came on a horse and said, "We're going to have a big storm tonight." So my husband said, "Do you think we should go to Manteo?" But he said, "No, I don't think so. You old Nags Headers should be all right." But my husband, of course, wanted to go right to Manteo. But I said, "No, I've always wanted to see a storm at Nags Head."

People came from the sound over to the ocean, and it was still and beautiful. We went on and had supper, and along about nine o'clock, the ocean kept getting bigger and bigger and bigger. The front door went down, and the ocean came right through it.

My husband, John Hall, picked up the baby, two and a half years old, and we waded in ocean water up above our waists, John Hall carrying the baby, over to the boarding house next door, which was further back from the ocean than our cottage. My sister, who was there keeping house, wouldn't leave her dog, so she stayed there all night. It never knocked it all the way down, but it damaged it badly.

There were a lot of people in the boarding house— at least thirty people. All night long it roared, and the cooks in the kitchen sang all night long. You could hear the sound of the wind and the music, the pouring-down rain and the wind blowing.

I was soaking wet from head to foot. I told John Hall to go back to the cottage and get me some dry clothes, and all he could find was a cocktail dress. I was glad to have anything dry.

Mrs. Worthington said, "We've all come safely through the night. I think we should say a prayer and thank the Lord." Well, she had nevermore said that, and I guess it was a tidal wave came crashing through the windows. It was pitch-black dark.

My baby was asleep on the cot, and I picked her up and held her up above my waist. My husband had gone out, and he came rushing in. They said he took an icebox off the porch and busted in the windows to see how we were. He picked up the baby, and he went out, and we waded to the road, and the water had washed under it. It was a bare thing. You had to grab hold of it and pull yourself up on the road.

I was pregnant at the time, but I didn't think a thing about it.

My sister stayed there the whole time with her dogs. We made it to the sound side and went to the Hathaway Cottage and all took refuge there. I don't know how many people were there. But they were all so tired. They fixed breakfast for us, then the wind shifted and the sound came up, and we moved to the Hollowell Cottage.

When it was over, it was over. The wind shifted and went the other way; the ocean died down. The next day, somebody brought us a car.

The people next door were amazed that we went to the sound side; they didn't think we should do that.

You know, I don't remember being scared. I always wanted to see a storm at Nags Head, but I don't ever want to see another one.

"He invited himself."
A president comes to Nags Head

PRESIDENT FRANKLIN DELANO ROOSEVELT RIDES IN HIS PACKARD ON THE WAY TO
NAGS HEAD FOR LUNCH WITH THE BUCHANAN FAMILY, AUGUST 18, 1937.
Courtesy of the Outer Banks History Center

While most summer days were spent accumulating sand between fingers and toes, a visit by the thirty-first president of the United States on the 350th anniversary of Virginia Dare's birth had Nags Headers lining the beach road to get a glimpse of their first real celebrity.

It was a humid afternoon—August 18, 1937—when Franklin Delano Roosevelt, on his way to see Paul Green's outdoor drama, *The Lost Colony*, stopped by for lunch in Nags Head. John Adams Buchanan, a Durham insurance executive, had built one of the largest cot-

tages on the beach the year before. The Buchanans were asked to host the president between his noontime docking in Manteo and the play that evening on Roanoke Island.

In the days before his visit, Nags Head children watched as workers sent by the White House built a ramp from the Buchanans' drive up to the back porch. On the day of his arrival, a crowd gathered along the beach road and on cottage porches nearby as the president's Packard came into view. In a flurry, mem-

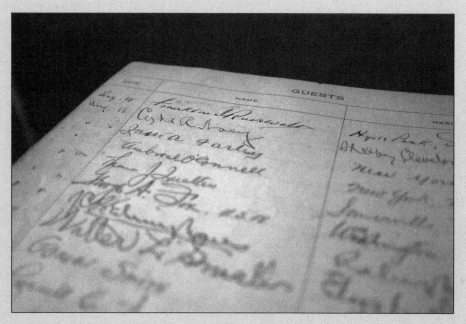

THE SIGNATURE OF PRESIDENT FRANKLIN DELANO ROOSEVELT (TOP LEFT) MADE IN THE BUCHANAN GUEST BOOK ON AUGUST 18, 1937
GOVERNOR CLYDE HOEY, FORMER GOVERNOR J. C. B. EHRINGHAUS, AND WALTER SMALL OF ELIZABETH CITY,
WHO ALL JOINED THE PRESIDENT FOR LUNCH, ALSO SIGNED THE BOOK.

Photo by Drew Crawford Wilson

bers of the White House staff brought a large oak chair into the house just before Roosevelt walked up the ramp, holding on to the railing.

Mary Frances Buchanan Flowers was a teenager at the time of the president's visit. She recalls how it came about.

We had a brand-new house. My aunt Mary Toms had just married Eddie Cameron, and we'd had the wedding at the house. It rained so hard that day that we had to put adhesive tape on the ceiling to keep the rain off the wedding cake. We were recuperating from the wedding when the White House called Mother to see if we could host the president for lunch and provide him a place to rest. He invited himself.

We didn't know him at all; my parents didn't even vote for him. But it was no burden. Mother and Daddy weren't political people at all. They liked him as a person, though they questioned what he was doing. He was a charming man.

I was eighteen years old when Roosevelt came for lunch. Five servants served lunch for fifty prominent

people and about thirty security people. Somebody from the White House came down and built a ramp, then Roosevelt drove up and got out of the car and with strong arms pulled himself up the ramp. He didn't want anybody to know he was in a wheelchair. My parents and I sat at a card table with him so he could use the wheelchair. He was so gracious.

The neighbors were standing all around on their porches, trying to see what was going on, but they weren't allowed inside our house. After he left, you've never seen such a crowd. They wanted to come and see what was going on.

Our servant—her real name was Sarah Jane Mary Ann John Down Christiana Perry, but we called her "Baa"—sat on the porch wearing a frilled white organdy cap Mother had made for her and a long uniform that hung to her ankles. She sat and waited to shake hands with her president. Baa was so sweet. She never knew how to read. We tried to teach her. She had so much common sense. She came to work with us when she retired at sixty-five after working her life in the tobacco fields.

When Roosevelt came in, he wanted a drink of something. We were Methodists, and my mother didn't serve alcohol in our home. Governor Hoey was there, too, and he was a teetotaler. But Daddy set up a bar on the second floor, and somehow they got a drink down to the president.

They didn't require Mother to submit a menu. They didn't come into the kitchen to taste the pots to see if they were poison. We served ham, of course, and a baked crabmeat, and our cook made the best rolls in the world. After lunch, the president went out on the front porch to look at the ocean and sat with my father.

While he was resting, the naval and army aides who came with him wanted to swim, but they didn't have bathing suits. So we called two of the servants, and they wore the servants' wool suits.

We have pictures in our beach pajamas and a guest book with his signature in it. Before he left, he called for all the servants to come out on the porch. He shook hands with each one and invited them to come to the White House.

"It wasn't sealed off from black people."
A servant talks of Nags Head

BEULAH WADSWORTH AND A FRIEND
ENJOY THE SURF IN THE 1940s.
Courtesy of Beulah Wadsworth

It was rare for a Nags Head family to spend summer at the beach without household servants to care for the children and cook the meals. From the 1830s, when those first Nags Head families brought household slaves to the beach, until well into the 1960s, when paid help spent the summer in maids' quarters, there was always a strong black community on the beach.

Beulah Wadsworth of Edenton spent her first summer at Nags Head in 1940 with the George Wood family. In later years, she worked for the family of the Reverend Fred Drane, son of Dr. Robert Brent Drane and uncle of Jaquelin Nash. Fred Drane, like his father, was rector of St. Andrew's-by-the-Sea. Beulah cared for several generations of Nags Head children, though she never learned to swim.

My mother died when I was twelve and left three under me, three boys. One was just three years old. I was the onliest one at the house. I couldn't go to school. I had to stay there and cook, keep house, and raise my brothers. I'd pump water, cut wood, wash on

the washboard, chop in the field, feed the chickens. My father was a farmer, but he had to do day's work out to support the family.

After I got married, I was the granny of Locust Grove. I kept all the children during the holidays for the parents to buy presents for them. There were twelve or thirteen houses then; now, there are only two.

The first time I went to Nags Head was in 1940 with Mrs. George Wood and her sister. I had never seen the ocean. We went down there on the ferry. They pulled the cars. I was scared and didn't ever get out. But the children would.

I'd heard so much about Nags Head, how they'd swim, about the cottages and everything. Where we put in, when we went to where the cottage was, the sound and the ocean met. We enjoyed being there. There were these big houses facing the water. The houses were high up. I didn't know how to swim—just stayed about ankle deep, where I could crawl.

It wasn't sealed off from black people. I didn't own a bathing suit. It was one they gave me from the cottage. I went in the ocean in the late afternoon. My grandson saw this picture and said it's a good thing they don't wear bathing suits like that now, we be done drowned. Where I was, all of us, white and black, mingled on the beach; we had no special time.

Back then, they all went to church at a certain time. But we didn't go to church there. We was working. There was no pleasure. But between lunch and supper, if we wanted to go swimming, we could go. Nobody bothered us. Sometimes, they would pass by, and we would talk.

After lunch, they would take us to ride, all around Nags Head. Stop by someplace and shop—the post office, the lighthouse.

Later on, I went with Mrs. Fred Drane. We had a kitchen, dining room. A porch would be all the way round the house. I had a nice big room right on the back. Mrs. Drane, whenever we was down there, they made it convenient for us, didn't put us out like no pigs or nothing. Wherever they sat and ate, that's where we sat. They made us available to everything that was in the house.

Mrs. Drane would say, "Come on, Beulah, let's go to ride." Sometimes, I'd go. Sometimes, I wouldn't. By then, I had about five children to take care of at the beach. They paid us more when we went to the beach.

Mr. Drane would have prayer meeting before breakfast every morning. On Sundays, they went to church, and when they got back home, I'd have the table set, the food cooked for fifteen people sometimes. By then, I did all the cooking. Mrs. Inglis—Mrs. Drane's daughter—would help me cook.

There was a [play] there that they called The Lost Colony. We went out there one night. It was a long building that had seats and a top over it. The act was people dressed up in all this stuff. About people lost. Mrs. Wood gave us money to go, and the chauffeur drove us. I had never seen it before. There was singing and dancing.

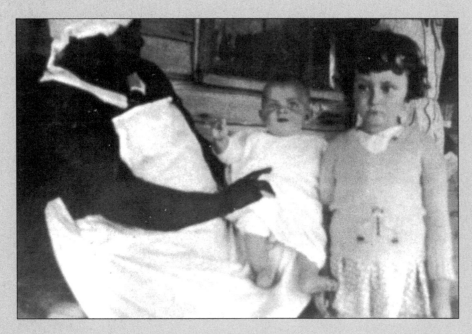

NURSEMAID HARRIET GRAHAM HOLDS BABY FRANCES DRANE IN 1929, WHILE THE BABY'S SISTER REBECCA STANDS AT HER SIDE. SERVANTS WERE FIXTURES ON THE BEACH FROM SOUND-SIDE DEVELOPMENT THROUGH THE 1970S.
Courtesy of Francis Drane Inglis

In the evening, the ocean was so pretty, the wind blowing, . . . always a nice breeze. When I first went down there, I couldn't half sleep, for I was scared of the water. But after I was there a couple of days, I got on it; it didn't bother me. I'd lay there and was gone in a minute.

I had a friend down there named Miss Mary Paxton. She was down there with the Williamses. I would go over to her house, because she was kind of old. She

couldn't half walk in that sand. There was one cottage between me and her, the Winslows'. After I'd get the dinner dishes washed up, I'd go round the back to her kitchen, and we'd sit and talk and laugh.

There was a fellow that would come down there fishing named Billy Pruden, and he'd throw a net out. When he'd drag it in, we'd go down and pick out the prettiest spot and croaker and things like that. I went back and got a big panful of croakers. I had to clean them, but we had them for supper.

We used to love to sit out on the porch and watch the ocean. One time, something was in the water as big as a cow, and it slid up and down like that—a porpoise. Once, we saw a small whale, a big, long thing. When I saw that, I was ready to come home. The war was going on along then, and I didn't know if the Germans had put a submarine coming up or what. Back then, we had curtains we'd pull down. The current went out, but we had candles and lanterns. Sometimes, we'd walk out at night, but I was scared. In some places, there was no light.

One time, we went to the lighthouse. We went to the museum first and looked at a lot of seashells and boats and guns. The children wanted to go up. There were a hundred steps, going round and round. When we got to the top, the children wanted to bounce all around, but I shooed them right on away from there, said to get on back, because if you fall down, that'd get you. We could see the ocean and the sound. It looked like I could almost see back home. It looked like the sky had come right down into the water.

Neap Tide

AERIAL VIEW OF THE UNPAINTED ARISTOCRACY IN THE 1940S
KESSINGER'S STORE IS LOCATED TO THE LEFT OF CENTER AND HOLLOWELL'S HOTEL IS TO THE RIGHT.

Courtesy of the Outer Banks History Center

> Neap tide, n. A tide occurring shortly after the first and third quarters of the moon, in which the high-water level stands at its lowest point; without power.
>
> *The Oxford*
> *English Dictionary*

III. NEAP TIDE: COMING OF AGE, 1950-1969

THE WAR WAS OVER and a new decade had come, yet most things about Nags Head continued as they had for close to a hundred years. By now, the houses constructed by S. J. Twine and other Nags Head builders numbered close to sixty, and a community of families bound to each other by a century of tradition inhabited them from May until September.

Though the world around them embraced twentieth-century technology, few, if any, of the cottages had television sets or telephones. But a fourth generation of Nags Headers didn't seem to mind, absorbed in the summer society run by mothers and aunts.

Betty Wales Howison now brought her three sons with her to Nags Head. "My friends still came," she remembers. "We wanted all our children to know each other like we did. I can't explain it. It just gets in your blood." And she didn't discard her childhood habit of kicking off her shoes at the back door as soon as she arrived. "It's not summer unless you go barefoot on the beach."

The children of the 1950s followed family custom, throwing off their shoes in the car at the first sight of the bridge over the Roanoke Sound. They'd jump from the car, then run to the ocean without stopping—just like parents and grandparents before them—to see if the Atlantic was just as they remembered. They played spades on the porch on quiet afternoons and took mandatory rests after lunch before diving back into the ocean. And before they'd head in for the day, they were sure to clean the beach tar—a remnant of the war just ended—from their feet with the kerosene-coated rag plugged into a Coca-Cola bottle on the front steps of every house.

Though the area was more populated now with vacationers renting beach boxes that stretched along the sand from Nags Head to Kitty Hawk, the families entrenched on Cottage Row held fast. Mothers came with the children, and fathers drove down on Friday afternoons.

Though they were fewer in number, uniformed servants who lived in quarters set off from the house still catered to the children and cooked for the families. In the morning, the servants walked the beach, scavenging for shells with the children and watching them as they played along the shoreline, careful not to let their charges venture into the breakers, since few servants even in the 1950s and 1960s knew how to swim. Summer still meant hard work for the servants, some of whom brought their own families with them to the beach. But when the children took their afternoon naps, there usually was time for servants to relax, socialize, and dip their toes into the water to cool off.

As ever-increasing numbers of new Nags Headers embraced the concept of a week-long summer vacation, the families in the old cottages kept their summer to themselves. Few of them could imagine, as they watched the sun set and lights flicker in the rental cottages that now surrounded them, how anyone could possibly stay in Nags Head for only a week.

The children of the 1930s indoctrinated their offspring into all that was Nags Head—Jockey's Ridge, St. Andrew's-by-the-Sea, the vast Atlantic, the cottages that housed generations of memories.

Jaquelin Nash brought her four children to Nags Head. The Buchanan sisters filled their house with children from their five families. Together with other Cottage Row families, they continued the rituals that had begun long before any of them was born. Dee Read and her sister, who used to lie in their beds on summer nights and find "pictures" in the wall and ceiling knotholes of their grandfather's cottage, now taught their children where to look for the chick hatching out of the egg. They relished teaching the youngest Nags Headers about the cottage they loved, pointing to the creaking step that used to give them up when they tried to sneak past their parents, and the favorite hole into which they always swept sand from the porch.

"My great-aunt Nannie Skinner used to say that when she died, she hoped heaven would be Nags Head," says Florence Nash of Durham, Jaquelin Nash's daughter. For Florence, a Durham poet, Nags Head is a potpourri of scents—her grandmother's Yardley Violet perfume, Noxzema, Absorbine Jr., sand, and salt.

Aunt Nannie, the Reverend Dr. Robert Drane's sister-in-law, lived her whole unmarried life with the Drane family. Long dead by the time Florence Nash began her Nags Head summers, Aunt Nannie was a presence nonetheless, her spirit drifting through the

corners of the house like a salty breeze.

Nannie Skinner loved the ocean. Every day, she would don her navy serge bathing suit and bob up and down in the water. She never got her hair wet, but drenched her body in the breakers. Then she'd head inside to dry off. Florence and her siblings spent many summer nights outside the cottage trading ghost stories, which always included the tale of the ghost of Aunt Nannie.

"I never knew her, but my older brother did," Florence Nash recalls. "She was very deaf, and she had an old-fashioned ear trumpet—a cow horn. She would sit in the living room with [it]. The most famous story was that my brother, when he was little, crept up to her side, putting his mouth on the ear trumpet, and screamed at Aunt Nannie.

"We kind of believed she lived in the attic. There was a square hole in the ceiling of one of the bedrooms below the attic, and we always thought she was up there looking at you. My brother would summon the courage to go up there, but I never did. In the old stairwell, the sand would drift downstairs and leave marks on the stairs. We always thought they were made by Aunt Nannie's skirts. My mother would say, 'Doesn't it cheer you up to know she's here? She's not a scary ghost.'

"My parents always worked against the fear. If there was a thunderstorm, they'd take us out on the porch and say, 'Isn't it beautiful?' And they'd tell us all sorts of stories about how wonderful thunder and lightning were. It was a wonder we didn't drown under the big waves, because they always told us we could jump under them. Everybody else would be snatching their children out of the water, and we would be jumping through the waves."

Whenever she recalls her teenage years, Florence sees Nags Head. "When I think about love and drama," says Florence, "I recall the sound of somebody's heavy footsteps on the porch after dark, and the tapping on the screened door. Then you'd walk on the dark beach, and especially if there was phosphorus, when the water is cold and the sand is cold, you'd dip your feet in the phosphorus, and they would glow. . . . Nothing in real life is as heightened as that toxic level of romance."

For the Buchanan sisters, christening their children

in the Nags Head experience meant bringing the whole family down together for fishing, storytelling, and games, tucking the children to sleep under mosquito nets in dormitory-style rooms paneled with beaded juniper.

Nags Head was in its heyday when Randy Coupland of Raleigh, son of Mary Frances Flowers's sister Susan, was growing up there in the 1950s and 1960s. "At the first sign of water," he says, "I'd roll the window down and smell the salt water."

Coupland's memories are ripe with pictures of his mother and aunts fishing in front of the cottage, each wearing one of the many hats that hung on a driftwood rack in the front hall. The stretch of beach in front of the Buchanan Cottage had a reputation for luring spot and bluefish; few days passed without the Buchanan sisters setting out their rods just after breakfast.

"My father taught me how to fish," says Coupland. "I remember standing next to him as he taught me how to bait a hook. We could stand there all day and fish and not catch a one, but it didn't matter. He was meticulous about his tackle box, keeping everything labeled in green plastic bags."

Through the open windows of the Buchanan Cottage, visitors could see a card table set up in the living room, newspapers dripping down its sides, four or five fishing rods angling like fingers across its top.

Coupland's grandfather Buchanan had enough grandsons to field a baseball team, and they held games in the afternoons in the sand on the street side of the house. On any given day, over a dozen boys from Nags Head's Cottage Row would line up to bat. Buchanan's driver, James, served as catcher.

"There was a closet at the back door that had everything in it for baseball," Coupland says. "I remember my grandfather pitching the ball to us; he loved it. He had an old black leather glove with flexible fingers. We used the chair cushions from the porch as bases. All the kids wanted to win. It was a guys' game."

Whether the activity was fishing or playing baseball on the sand, the center was the house, and family was its heart.

For the children of the 1950s and 1960s, Nags Head was still an expanse of clean sand and sea oats. Florence Nash and her cousins would occupy themselves for hours with leftover juniper shingles and a magnifying glass, writing their names in script with the help of concentrated sunlight. "You could lose yourself in something like that all day," she says.

But those who now roamed the dunes at Nags Head had more options. They could escape the heat in a movie theater in Manteo, head to the Casino for bowling—or dancing, if they were old enough—or play miniature golf at a new course just across the road. Still, as their parents and grandparents before them, they all climbed Jockey's Ridge, which had shifted slightly but was still the East Coast's tallest dune. And playing under the house remained a favored pastime, despite the passing of years.

LEFT: JOHN ADAMS BUCHANAN, SEATED IN THE CENTER OF THE SECOND ROW FROM THE TOP, IS SURROUNDED BY HIS FIVE DAUGHTERS AND THEIR HUSBANDS AND CHILDREN. THE PHOTOGRAPH WAS TAKEN ON THE FRONT STEPS OF THEIR COTTAGE AT NAGS HEAD IN THE 1950s.

Courtesy of Randy Coupland, seated in the front to the far right

BELOW: AERIAL VIEW OF NAGS HEAD IN THE EARLY 1950s ST. ANDREW'S-BY-THE-SEA IS LOCATED IN THE CENTER OF THE PHOTOGRAPH.

Courtesy of the Outer Banks History Center

"We used to build a whole city of foxholes under the house [using] sand, sea grass, and driftwood," says John "Possum" Silver, Betty Howison's son. "We stole cigarettes and smoked 'em under there. My cousins used to smoke cigars."

"I remember one time my children planned a sleepover with their friends, and they all wanted to sleep under the house," Dee Read recalls. "They all got under there and got to telling ghost stories. Well, the maid's daughter was under there with them, and she fell fast asleep. They all got scared and came into the house—all except for that little girl. She was sound asleep. We went under the house in the night and got her and brought her into the house."

Attending church on Sunday was the one thing the children still were expected to do. It remained the only day a Nags Head child was required to wear shoes.

"On Sunday morning, we had to get up and put on shoes our feet didn't fit, and a nice dress," Florence Nash recalls. "And we only put them on when we got on the far side of the road. But it was a small offering of gratitude for our privilege of being there. In a way, church was our penance. But the church was where everybody came together. It was so perfect and plain and beautiful. It stood up out of the sand. And inside, the windows were usually open. You'd sit in the pew, and you could see Engagement Hill and sky and dune. There were always sea oats in the pewter altar vases. All the hymns were twice as nice."

The rules that Jaquelin Nash learned as a child were now nailed kid's-eye high on the cottage door to greet her children: Don't talk about disgusting things at the table; never leave the house without telling a grownup; hang up your bathing suit or you can't go swimming; everyone must be silent for one hour after lunch.

The Casino continued to attract summer dancers, who now came from all over eastern North Carolina to hear the bands. But Ras Wescott himself was the dominant figure at the Casino, no matter who was playing on stage. Though he hired bouncers with bodies as big as tree trunks to keep order each night, Wescott shared that responsibility. He stood six feet tall and constantly surveyed the dance floor, making sure no beer left the tables. He made it his business to know everyone who entered the Casino, and he knew their ages, too.

"Ras sent many a young person to college who might not have gone," says Donnie Twyne of Manteo, former police chief of Nags Head and a Casino legend in his own right. "He treated me like a father."

Twyne was twelve years old in 1933 when he got his first job at the Casino, setting up duckpins on the first floor. Later, he moved behind the bar. When Twyne became chief of police, he spent many nights patrolling the Casino's parking lot, on the watch for trouble.

"It was a rough place," Twyne recalls. "It could hold two thousand people. They came from all over—Hampton, Windsor, Tarboro, Elizabeth City, Hertford. There was nowhere else to go. A lot of people hated it, but ten times more loved it. I don't care if the world goes on; the Casino will never be forgotten."

Donnie Twyne, folks contend, was not afraid of lightning. Stories circulated through the years of Twyne's arresting thirty people in one night, corralling them three at a time into his patrol car. One night, a disorderly patron jumped out one of the large, open windows that ran along both sides of the dance hall. Twyne jumped out right behind him and chased him up Jockey's Ridge. He also claims that, another time, he arrested the ambassador to the Netherlands, handcuffing him and taking him to jail.

But Twyne is not the only colorful character from the Casino's history. Others like him made their living watching over the place. There was Umphie Cox, a black waiter who lived in the barracks Wescott provided behind the Casino. Miss Delnoy Burrus took tickets each night, with Beauty, her Pekingese, at her side, guarding the stairs that led to the second-floor dance hall. Reportedly, the dog would "speak" to everyone who came into the Casino, unless they'd been drinking beer before they arrived. Wescott's own dog, a German shepherd named Satan, loved Coca-Cola and would dance across the floor on his hind legs whenever his owner said the word. Among the dancers everyone remembers was Theresa Beasley. Once, the tale is told, she danced on the ceiling while her partner danced on the floor. Some folks came just to watch her, or to have a chance to dance with her. Teenagers may not have known how to dance the first time they came to the Casino, but they learned all the moves by watching dancers like Theresa glide across the floor.

Twenty years after World War II, more change transformed the placid beach. In the early 1960s, the state built a new highway, N.C. 158 Bypass, which stretched the eastern side of the barrier island from the Currituck bridge in the north to Whalebone Junction in the south. Within a few short years, fast-food restaurants sprouted along its edges, bringing what some saw as convenience to Nags Head, though the cottagers had a much different view.

As in other times, the weather continued to be a factor in shaping Nags Head. Early on the morning of March 7, 1962—Ash Wednesday, the beginning of the Christian season of penitence—two storms, one from the west and one from the east, converged over the Outer Banks and moved northward. Though only a small accumulation was forecast, snow fell as far south as Alabama. Three inches were recorded in areas inland toward Elizabeth City. Ice, sleet, and snow pelted the area north and west of the Albemarle Sound and moved west, blanketing much of the state.

Winds of more than seventy-five miles per hour assaulted the Nags Head beachfront. The ocean came ashore for the next several days in a great fury, producing the highest of tides—a spring tide—which brought with it mountains of sand that found refuge

A PATTERN OF ANGLES AND LINES

THE FRED P. WOOD COTTAGE, PRUDEN-BATTLE-CLARK COTTAGE, AND WOOD-FOREMAN COTTAGE AT SUNSET

Photo by Drew Crawford Wilson

inside many houses of the Unpainted Aristocracy. Water levels near Midgett's Store reached six feet; close to thirty inches of sea found its way inside the store.

Donnie Twyne, who was then Nags Head's chief of police, had been sleeping in the highway patrol station along N.C. 12 when he woke up to find water flooding the premises. Wading outside into the raging northeaster, he found his brand-new police car just where he'd parked it, though it was now submerged in choppy ocean water. He set out for higher ground. Jockey's Ridge was not far away, but he decided to head south. He crawled out of the water more than a mile away, south of St. Andrew's-by-the-Sea.

A decade earlier, when N.C. 158 Bypass was in the planning stages, Carmen Gray's grandfather Jethro Midgett had warned engineers that if the highway were built above sea level, it would serve as a dike, trapping the sea between the highway and the oceanfront dune line, should there be a flood. Until the highway was built, whenever there was a flood, the ocean washed over the flats and into the sound before it drained away. But what Midgett predicted came to be in the early hours of that Ash Wednesday, as the entire area around the old cottages flooded. The tides were so strong that portions of the bypass washed away, leaving gaping holes in the road. Water flooded Jigsaw Road, which connected the oceanfront to the sound; now, where the road once stood, a river of salt water rushed toward the sound in a giant wave, taking pieces of the Jigsaw with it. The cottages fared little better. A few were destroyed. Others lost sides and porches. Sand collected under the cottages, so those that had been five feet off the ground were now sitting on it.

"My uncle took my grandmother in a dory over to the highest dune," Carmen Gray recalls, "which was near the Baptist church, and he put her on a helicopter with my dog, Duchess. They took her to Manteo, where she had friends. I was a teacher, and we didn't go to school for a long time. They had just put in a new floor in the store, and it buckled."

Because it was winter, most of the cottages were empty. But news of the devastation spread around the region, so that within a few days of the storm, the owners began to trickle in to see what damage had been done.

"We were in Raleigh at the time," recalls Betty Howison, who has a pillow in her cottage living room that reads, "Nothing works in an old cottage except the owner."

"My brother and his wife came and picked up my husband and me. It was March eighth. When we got to Nags Head, we crossed the bridge, and we had to walk a long way. The sand was like quicksand, and there was lots of water everywhere. It was so quiet, it was eerie.

"When we saw the cottage, the front porch had come off, and the back porch was in the sand. We cried so hard we laughed. There were other summer people there. We all said, 'Look what's happened to you.'

"When we went inside, the sand had come all the way through the walls. There were piles of sand in the front three rooms. The pressure of the sand had dislocated the floor. The dining-room table had been turned over, and the legs were up against the ceiling.

"We wondered how quick we could put it back together. It hadn't been moved until then, but we picked it up, moved it back, and put new pilings under it. The Prudens next door found Mr. Hare to move it, and he went into the business. We were back to business in June."

Winds were clocked at seventy-six miles per hour; though hurricane winds begin at seventy-five miles per hour, the storm was classified as a northeaster.

"After the Ash Wednesday Storm," says Dee Read, "nobody was here all summer. I was walking down the beach, and the cottages all looked like open-sided dollhouses, their curtains blowing out of the windows in the wind. Everybody was waiting in line for the movers."

∽

During the 1960s, summer for many teenagers along the cottage line meant finding work at Nags Head, rather than staying inland. Randy Coupland landed a job as an alley boy at the Casino, setting up pins in the downstairs bowling alley while beach music sifted down from the dance hall upstairs. When he was a little older, he joined the ranks of pink-tuxedoed waiters at the Seafare Restaurant, a relatively new Nags Head establishment. He surfed during the day,

waited tables at night, then slept in the waiters' barracks away from his family's cottage for the first time. "I always knew I'd be at Nags Head," he says.

Ras Wescott continued to bring some of the most popular bands in the Southeast to the Casino. The Jitterbug had evolved into the Shag by now. The Chairmen of the Board sang "Give Me Just a Little More Time" as barefoot dancers in Bermuda shorts and madras shirts took them to heart and shagged into the early-morning hours. Black bands like the Tams, the Drifters, the Four Tops, Doug Clark and the Hot Nuts, and Maurice Williams and the Zodiacs continued to draw college audiences to the dance floor.

Though the world around it was soon to be caught up in the civil-rights movement, the Casino remained a white establishment. When black bands played the Casino, their guests couldn't enter by the front door and were sequestered at a special table to one side of the stage. Many of the servants who had been coming to Nags Head since the 1940s and 1950s enjoyed the bands, too, though they were not allowed inside the Casino. Often, they would gather across the street on the porches of the cottages' maids' quarters and listen as the music they loved drifted out the open windows and into the dark.

Around 1967, Bill Deal and the Rondells, a white "copy band" from Virginia Beach, ventured down to the Casino for their first summer. Though they weren't a traditional beach-music band, the Rondells took a stab at playing tunes that the locals were used to hearing, but to their own beat. Within a year, they were recording their own records and were listed on the *Billboard* Top 100 with a hit, "May I?" they "copied" from Maurice Williams, who had played it at the Casino.

By the end of the 1960s, the world that surrounded the Unpainted Aristocracy was swirling into motion. Long-haired surfers, drawn to the Outer Banks by the waves, were eager to get into the Casino, but Wescott kept them out, establishing a new hair-length rule. Delnoy Burrus was rumored to keep a pair of scissors with her at all times; it was said that, on more than one occasion, she cut the ponytail off a patron eager to gain entry into the legendary dance hall.

Long hair on teenagers was only one sign of the changing world. And while those carefree summer days made it almost possible to forget that the country was immersed in a war, Nags Headers would see their most visible sign that the world was changing before the end of the decade.

On July 20, 1969, the waxing crescent moon that lingered over Nags Head was the center of attention. Since few cottagers had televisions, and since reception was snowy at best, some of Nags Head's children gathered in a cottage in Kill Devil Hills to watch man's first walk on the moon.

Their parents had a front-row seat at Wright Brothers National Memorial, where a special television hookup had been arranged. But no matter where they witnessed Neil Armstrong's leap from the ladder of the lunar module, few Nags Headers who saw the moon that night could help marveling at how different their world had become.

Looking out to the sea from the porch of the MacMullan Cottage, originally known as the George D. Poole Cottage
Photo by Drew Crawford Wilson

"It was like magic."
Bill Deal and the Rondells

THE NAGS HEAD CASINO IN THE 1950S
Courtesy of The Outer Banks History Center

Mention the Nags Head Casino to anyone over forty-five and their eyes drift easily into a favorite beach memory. No matter whether they hail from the era of Tommy Dorsey and Glen Miller or the Temptations and Maurice Williams, most view the Nags Head Casino as the icon of their summer lives. For over forty years, dancers and music lovers from all corners of eastern North Carolina and Tidewater Virginia gathered in the concrete building that sat on a thin strip of parking lot just across from Jockey's Ridge. There, they heard some of the biggest bands in the country. Everybody, it seemed, played the Casino.

Few have been changed more dramatically by the Casino than Bill Deal, "Fat" Ammons Tharp, and their band, Bill Deal and the Rondells. A Virginia Beach "copy band" that began playing together in the late 1950s, the

Rondells made their first trip to the Casino in the 1960s. That trip led to many others. One balmy night, the Rondells played a song at the Casino that would change their lives forever. Bill Deal remembers those summers and that song.

Our band had been playing together since we were in college, since about 1959. Ras Wescott was keen about the entertainment that he booked. Beginning around 1965, we would play there once every six or seven weeks, rotating with bands like Maurice Williams and the Zodiacs, JoJo and the Frets, and the Rocking Cabanas, and many I'm leaving out. The bouncers at the Casino were as big as tree trunks. When we performed, Ras was always walking all through the place, keeping an eye on the kids.

We'd rent the brown Bell Cottage close to the Casino. In those first few years, I'd bring my family, and we'd be booked for five days. We got to learn the crowd. We were just kids when we first went to Nags Head; it was probably our first venture into travel. I could only imagine the history there; I didn't really know it. . . .

We were a Virginia Beach band. I was at Old Dominion, and my wife was about to have our first child. We were what they call a copy band; we'd play the hits, play the beach music, whatever the crowd wanted to hear. It was always packed. We never worried about not having a crowd.

Quite by chance, the crowd wanted to hear this song, "May I?"—a song Maurice Williams wrote and would

perform when he was there. They already loved Maurice Williams. He'd been playing there for a few years. But we just didn't play that kind of music up here, that hard-core beach music. I'd heard it before and thought, "We can't do that." It was laid-back beach music.

But you play what the crowd wants to hear, and they wanted "May I?" We hadn't practiced it. The way we did music back then, I'd listen to it, and I'd sketched out the base line, the horns and piano, and Ammons

DANCERS TAKE TO THE FLOOR IN THE 1940s.
Courtesy of The Outer Banks History Center

would pick up on the drums. Without even rehearsing it, we did it. I listened to it in the car and wrote out the notes. We used a polka beat, kind of making fun of it and kind of not.

It was almost like a big fraternity and sorority party, and when we played it, the crowd was screaming at us. We looked at each other and thought, "Man, that felt good." We probably played it three times that first night, which was very unusual. We knew maybe twenty-seven songs, so to play one three times, that was different. It felt so good. We decided that night to investigate recording.

That was 1967. That very week, we made a cold call to Warren Miller, who had a small studio in Norfolk, and recorded "May I?" It was like magic. Nothing else we did really sounded like that. The um-pa, um-pa. We had no idea what would happen, but we liked the sound. We printed probably a thousand 45s, and they were gone within a week. We had to go back and print five thousand. Then a distributor called and wanted ten thousand.

By 1968, it was too big for us to handle. A disc jockey from WGH in Virginia Beach, Gene Loving, was contacted by MGM's Heritage Records. They'd heard about the song, which by now was a regional hit without national status. Gene and I made our first trip to New York, and I signed with MGM, and the next thing you know, we had five records that year, [including] "May I?", "I've Been Hurt," [and] "What Kind of Fool," three that charted very well. They were international hits as well. "I've Been Hurt" was the number-one song of the year for Mexico in 1969. I just did a deal last week with a company in Germany about these songs. And it all started at the Casino.

By the next year, when we played at the Casino, we had worked on our presentation, choreography, lighting. We were doing Dick Clark and shows like that, taking it to another level. The next time we played it, the kids were such a part of the song being what it was, it was amazing.

The Casino certainly opened doors for a lot of groups. It also gave us an opportunity to see other entertainers. I became friends with people like Freddie Owens and Gary Brown, two very strong entertainers. It was a showcase for bands. If you played the Casino, you'd made it.

People who love that beach music will not let it go. It may never get its page in Billboard, but it deserves more recognition than it gets. So many other types of music have come around since then, and most of the young people probably listen to that, but there is a hardcore beach-music element that still exists.

There is not a place like [the Casino] anymore. Things are so busy in every aspect of life. Those were such simple, easygoing days. You pretty much had your girl or your children or you were in school; that was a lot of people's lives. It was that simple.

But the Casino changed our lives. God bless them for making us do "May I?"

"I guess I thought they'd be here forever to tell it."
The Midgetts of Nags Head

A TREASURE OF TRINKETS
MATTIE MIDGETT DISPLAYS A WOODEN CARVING FROM HAITI, WHICH SHE FOUND ON THE BEACH.
Courtesy of Carmen Gray / Reproduced by Drew Crawford Wilson

Among the many memories that have shaped Nags Head's cottage families through the years are stories about the Midgett family. Mattie Midgett ran the local store, which first opened on the sound side, then later moved just across the street from the Buchanan Cottage next to the beach road. The Midgetts provided everything—fresh squash and tomatoes, croakers and blue crabs, ice-cold Coca-Colas. They even took phone calls, since the store phone was the only one on the island for many years. Though the store is closed today, it is occasionally opened for visitors, who marvel at the relics that Mattie Midgett's daughter, Nellie Myrtle, gleaned from years of beachcombing around Nags Head.

Carmen Gray, who now lives in Kitty Hawk, grew up behind her grandparents' store. She recalls how the family kept track of everything summer Nags Headers needed. A native Nags Header, Carmen's voice contains the remnants of the "hoi toid" accent long associated with natives of the Outer Banks.

My grandmother Mattie Twiford Midgett was the postmaster when Nags Head was known as Griffin. They called her Peach. She married Jethro Midgett in 1914 and worked there on the sound side in a store until the 1933 storm. Then they moved the store to the beach.

Granddaddy was a Midgett from Manns Harbor. I never heard that his family came from anywhere. They probably shipwrecked here. Peach's mother came from Elizabeth City.

Jethro's family owned the land from sea to sound right at the Wright memorial. They owned the hill. They sold it in the 1930s to Frank Stick and somebody else. Frank Stick sold it to the government in 1937.

Grandmother had the store. She was a lovely lady, a fat, round, little thing. She was loved by everybody. She could stand on her porch and shout, and we could hear her in the sound. We all minded her.

She kept ledgers in the store. Everybody had his page in the book for the summer. Most people only paid once a month. She'd itemize every bit of coffee, every loaf of bread and candy bar. We had one family, he and his wife would buy two eggs and three pieces of bacon. He was one of the richest men on the beach, but my God, was he tight. Even Granddaddy's net records, when he purchased the nets and sold fish to people, his records were well kept. Couldn't read his writing, but his records were right.

Granddaddy was a fisherman. He might have done a little bootlegging, too, like everybody. You know, I didn't pay much attention when I was growing up to anything that was told to me, because I didn't think it mattered. I guess I thought they'd be here forever to tell it.

The only interesting thing I remember about him is that Granddaddy had what was known as a "pound net," but it was not really a net. When he'd go fishing, he'd dump the fish in the pound, and the [women] would come stand on the dock and say, "Mr. Midgett, would you have your daughter go and get me so many flounders?" And they'd have the audacity to point to a flounder with my mother, Nellie Myrtle, down in there with those fish.

MATTIE MIDGETT KEPT METICULOUS RECORDS SHOWING EVERYTHING ANY NAGS HEAD FAMILY BOUGHT AT THE STORE. THIS LEDGER SHOWS THE ACCOUNT OF REVEREND DR. ROBERT BRENT DRANE, RECTOR OF ST. ANDREW'S-BY-THE-SEA. *Photo by Drew Crawford Wilson*

NELLIE MYRTLE MIDGETT WAS THE EPITOME OF A BEACHCOMBER. WITH A BAG TO COLLECT HER
TREASURES, SHE WOULD WALK THE SANDS OF NAGS HEAD DAILY. IN THIS PHOTOGRAPH, BOTTLES OF SHELLS
AND SEA GLASS, ALL GLEANED FROM THE BEACH, LINE THE SHELVES OF THE OLD STORE.
Photo by Drew Crawford Wilson

Uncle Jethro, Jr., ran the fish market. Before the fish market, he was the iceman. It would come over in three-hundred-pound cakes, and he would take his ice pick and block it off in a hundred pounds, a hundred pounds, then fifty, fifty. Then he'd put it in this army truck he had and put canvas over it, and he and half the girls on the beach would take around the ice. He was a handsome man. There were never any restrictions in those days. When he drove that truck with the ice in it, he drove it to everybody's house.

Kessinger's Store burned in the 1940s. There was a line—either a power line or a telephone line—that dropped, and everybody on the number-two line, I think it was, was on fire at the same time, including us. Charlie Martin's was on fire, and Peach's was on fire, the Buzzard Roost. Well, the fire truck had to come from

Manteo, and they didn't have but one. But there was somebody smart enough in our group to grab a rubber hose and throw it over that line and snatch it loose. It burned a hole in our floor. The ground was shocking you. Kessinger's was the only one that burned.

My grandfather pulled the dory boat with the army truck. The best fishing was right in front of the Buchanans', the line from the old Arlington Hotel to the Croatan [a hotel in Kill Devil Hills]. They fished from the spring until fall. People would come with their dishpans and buy fish right off the beach. Granddaddy had one beautiful garden, and he'd sell vegetables in the store.

The only telephone was at the store, and it was a hand-crank. If it was within distance of the Prudens' or the Buchanans', you could holler for them. Otherwise, we'd take a message. People waited in line to use it. They'd get in the phone booth and shut the door. Everybody called on Saturday night at nine o'clock. I was the Western Union girl and took all the telegrams and delivered them.

My mother, Nellie Myrtle, did a lot of soft-crabbing on the shore. She always crabbed with her toes. It was the most amazing thing. We could walk beside her and not catch a crab, but she would take her toes and move those tin cans and move those shingles, and she knew they were there. She'd pick that sucker up, and we couldn't see it to save our lives.

Nellie Myrtle did not appreciate the tourists, the attitudes, the fact that we were here as their servants, that when they asked us to jump, we would say, "How high?" That went against her grain. She had lots of things stopped, one being people who were taking the gravel off the beaches for their cement. She was a very bright lady and could have gotten an awful lot done if she'd had any finesse whatsoever. But she didn't have any. It was, "You do it my way or not at all."

She was a real beachcomber. She walked the beach every day and never left home without a plastic bag; I guess it was paper in the beginning. But she always knew she would find something. One of her favorite things to do was to pick up the bricks that the waves would unearth after storms—chimneys of bygone days. She used them around her flower beds. None would go to waste.

It was her beach. She didn't live on the beach, but she was the boss of everything. If there was a footprint in the winter, she called the police. She called them for everything. She saw what was happening to the beach, and she knew there wasn't going to be a piece of dirt left in the county, that it was going to be abused by all those who drove on the hills and drove on the beach. They came from elsewhere, and they didn't care about it or us. They were here to have a good time—fifteen or twenty of them at the time—and litter it with beer cans and crush all of her shells. She knew there was no way it was ever going to replenish. That's why she was so protective.

When she wasn't on the beach, she was on the hills plundering—the sand dunes out behind the Episcopal church, the Seven Sisters. We have some nice things that

MATTIE MIDGETT AND LATER NELLIE MYRTLE KEPT THEIR EYES ON THE UNPAINTED ARISTOCRACY FROM THESE FRONT-PORCH ROCKERS.

Photo by Drew Crawford Wilson

she found, little doll plates and one full china doll, lots of arrows, hatpins. Pin Hill, north of Jockey's Ridge, was where the seamstress lived. Her house burned down, and they called her a witch. There were all kinds of goodies that kept blowing up out there.

In the wintertime, duck hunters came down, and Granddaddy was a guide. He and my uncle built houses or reshingled them, worked with Mr. Twine some. There was always enough to eat.

When Mother died in July, we had her cremated. And we waited until everybody left the beach in September, then we had a memorial service at seven o'clock on the beach. [My son] Bill and Edward Reber, Jr., took her ashes out on the dory, and right then the wind changed. Those boys, I swear, almost drowned. It blew up the worst northeaster you have ever seen in your life. We had hyacinths in shells from her house that we tossed into the ocean. The dolphins came behind the boat, and five pelicans came down and gave her a salute.

It's over. There is no preservation left. The only preservation will be among those of us who think we're natives and are holding on somehow. But I don't know how we're going to hold up anything. Every piece of land is built on. When they advertise "the last piece of sand in Corolla," they don't know how bad that sounds to us. Everything is gone, all these wonderful things that didn't desecrate the ground that we remember. We played on Jockey's Ridge, and it must have been fifty feet high.

JETHRO MIDGETT, SR., A DORY FISHERMAN, SHARES A FISH WITH HIS GREAT-GRANDDAUGHTER, MONIQUE GRAY, IN THE 1960s.
Photo courtesy of Carmen Gray
Reproduced by Drew Crawford Wilson

It's no longer just us, and that's the saddest part. When it was just us, we could pretty well keep a handle on it and have a good time, too.

Spring Tide

FROM LEFT TO RIGHT: RUDGE KING, DAWSON RASCOE, AND PETER RASCOE III, ENJOY THE BEACH IN 1960.

Courtesy of J. Peter Rascoe III / Reproduced by Susan Byrum Rountree

IV. SPRING TIDE: CLINGING TO TRADITION, 1970-1989

J. PETER RASCOE III's Nags Head roots are deeper than most. Ancestors on both sides of his family vacationed here beginning in the mid-nineteenth century. His mother's great-great-grandfather was Francis Nixon, Nags Head's first vacationer. In 1908, his great-grandfather Thomas Nixon, who was also Dee Read's grandfather, acquired the Grandy Cottage, built in 1866 and now known as the Nixon Cottage. His father's grandfather Aaron Spivey Rascoe owned a hotel on the sound side. His mother's father, Brack Dawson, worked during the summers of his youth driving a cart from the sound to the beachfront. Dawson later built the Nags Header Hotel and the Nags Head Beach Club with his brothers.

During the 1960s, J. Peter Rascoe III spent every summer in the cottage built by his grandfather Rascoe in 1931 for fifteen hundred dollars. Located on the northern fringe of the Unpainted Aristocracy, the Rascoe Cottage sits just across the street from Jockey's Ridge, where N.C. 158 and the beach road almost meet. Though it's been moved twice, the original part of the gray structure hasn't changed in seventy years.

"Jethro Midgett looked after our cottage for my father," recalls Peter Rascoe, Jr., who grew up in Windsor. "After the '33 storm, Jethro got after my daddy to move it, said he'd better jack it up and move it back. Jethro finally convinced him in 1962, exactly thirty days before the Ash Wednesday Storm. That was the first time it was ever moved, and there wasn't really any damage to it."

The younger Rascoe, who grew up in his father's hometown, was raised by a family enraptured with its history. His parents now live in a restored plantation home on the Perquimans River in Hertford County; it was built by mother Nancy Dawson Rascoe's ancestors in 1815 on land acquired in 1812. As a child, J. Peter Rascoe III often accompanied his mother as she searched through old houses for wood and brick to use in the home she and her husband were building in Windsor.

Nags Head summers were a familiar thread in the family's life. Nancy Rascoe grew up in Elizabeth City and summered in her grandfather's Nixon Cottage. She met her future husband at Nags Head when she was eleven years old. As teenagers, they danced together at the Casino. They dated in college and married in 1956.

"My mother went down in 1908 to the Nixon Cottage when she was just two years old," says Nancy, who has spent years informally compiling a history of the area. "It was a way of life. They didn't go until the first of July because my grandfather farmed. But they played with all the same children, and we played with their children, and now our grandchildren are playing with theirs. That's the greatest strength of Nags Head. There is that bond all along the cottage line."

"The legacy was all around you, and you were reminded of it all the time," says Peter III, who was born in 1957. "The families on either side of you were very close, and probably at least third cousins. Crab-

bing and swimming, taking Jeep rides in Nags Head Woods, climbing Jockey's Ridge—we would hear our parents say they did the same things."

Like the rest of Nags Head's children, Peter packed up his belongings around Memorial Day. He then moved to the beach with his mother and two brothers. Like the other fathers, Peter Rascoe, Jr., joined his family on the weekends.

"When my friends went to summer camp," says Peter, "I can remember thinking, 'There's something else to do in the summertime,' but I couldn't imagine being anywhere else. There was always a lot of family, sometimes three generations at one time. I can still picture my grandmother May Bell Rascoe in the morning sitting out in the rocking chairs with her sister, on the front porch."

For the Rascoes, Nags Head summers meant living like their ancestors did in the old house. There was one bathroom on the porch, so everyone in the house—even the adults—used chamber pots during the night. The first chore for everyone in the family each morning was to empty their pot.

In the 1960s, servants still played an important role in the Rascoes' life. Carleigh Speller Moore, the black woman who had cared for Nancy as a child, joined the family every summer at Nags Head, now watching over her second generation of Dawson children.

"It was such a thrill to me that Carleigh raised me," says Nancy, "and then she'd come down on the bus and stay with me and my children. She could fry

fish. Big Peter learned to fry fish from her. We'd roast marshmallows and take watermelons out on the beach. They'd do the same thing we had done as children."

At night, Peter III joined others his age, playing flashlight tag on the beach or scrambling across the highway to climb Jockey's Ridge. As he grew older, he and his friends gathered at the top of a sand hill across from the Casino, scouring the dance club's open windows for a glimpse of what the older kids were doing inside. Ras Wescott, who by now had been hosting teenagers at the Casino for over thirty years, christened the hill Monkey World, in honor of the "mon-

keys" who converged there each night.

At the time, it all seemed like innocent fun. It would take growing older, visiting other beaches with friends, even moving away for Peter to discover that, for him, Nags Head was more than just a place to go to be away from home.

"One of my big memories is of lying in bed, listening to the ocean crashing," he says. "The windows were wide open to catch any breeze, the curtains billowing out. Now when I stay in a cottage off the beach, I have to strain to hear it. That's a premium that we all took for granted."

In the early 1970s, a change took place that began

the transformation of the Rascoe Cottage, pushing it toward the ways of the rest of the world. Grandfather Rascoe fell ill, and the family had a telephone installed in the cottage. They'd spent their summers without one for forty years.

A much more profound transformation came around that same time, when an Ocean City, Maryland, real-estate developer began marketing the Outer Banks as a vacationers' paradise. Tourists swarmed to the Outer Banks like flies in a land breeze. Suddenly, Nags Head and the surrounding beaches were dis-

covered. Weekly vacationers crowded the cottages that flanked the old Cottage Row, packing the once-quiet beaches. Strip shopping centers took root along the beach road and the bypass, their shouting billboards and neon signs overshadowing the quiet grays and browns that had long defined the area. Stoplights, fast-food restaurants, more shopping centers, and even a mall flooded the once-tranquil beach.

Jockey's Ridge felt the impact, too. Thousands of tourists continued to climb the dune each year, among them hang gliders who, in the spirit of the Wright

JOCKEY'S RIDGE

Photo by Drew Crawford Wilson

brothers, found the dune to be the ideal place to perfect their craft.

Though the dune had always been privately owned, many Nags Headers felt as though it belonged to them. Alarmed by the shifting sands and the flow of tourists to Jockey's Ridge, some residents—led by native Nags Header Carolista Fletcher Baum Golden—launched a campaign to create a state park. In 1975, the state acquired the land for Jockey's Ridge State Park.

The establishment of the state park dimmed some of the generations-old enthusiasm Nags Headers felt for climbing Jockey's Ridge. The cottage children had long since lost their privilege of combing the dune from dawn until dusk, with so many strangers there, and no one had been allowed to roast marshmallows or drive Jeeps on the summit in years.

The Casino was a casualty of the times, too. Ras Wescott had grown too old to continue running the dance hall, and it fell into disrepair. He sold it to investors, who transformed the landmark into a private club that did not continue the Casino's forty-year tradition of drawing crowds. In 1976, a northeaster that blew through Nags Head dropped so much rain that the roof of the old building collapsed. The structure was razed and in time was replaced by the behemoth headquarters for Kitty Hawk Kites, a center for the hang gliders who now took flight from the dune.

Cottage Row itself could not escape the impact of time and tides. Some of the old structures gave

way to the fury of the Atlantic. Other families sold their legacies to newcomers, who some Nags Headers felt had little appreciation for this area's history. Still others modernized, adding air conditioning and storm windows, which shut out the traffic noise but also the ocean winds.

And the ocean continued to pound the beach, taking enough sand with it to prompt property owners to jack up their cottages and move them closer still to the road.

Some cottagers, worried that the encroaching commercial growth would soon destroy the area, participated in an effort to have their historic beachfront listed on the National Register. Catherine Bishir, then head of the Survey and Planning Branch for Historic Preservation of the North Carolina Division of Archives and History, visited the beach at the request of a colleague. Within a short time, she set to work chronicling the architectural history of Cottage Row.

"What I saw at Nags Head was amazingly wonderful," says Bishir. "At the time, the concept of an historic district was in its early development. We were thinking of places like New Bern and Hillsborough— traditional districts—but most of the architecture at Nags Head was early twentieth century. Still, there were these great forms sitting in that line for a century. There was nothing like it anywhere. They reflected an architectural unity that was about the social unity of the place."

With the help of colleagues and Carolista Baum Golden, Bishir interviewed dozens of cottagers and researched the origin and architecture of the structures. As her work progressed, she became fascinated with the stories.

"I don't know what it is, but when these older people talked about Nags Head, they got younger in about five minutes. They had such clear memories that brought them such pleasure. I was so interested, I wanted it to be more than just defining the historic district. It is just an ordinary beach place; you have the cottage with the porch, then the ocean, and nothing in between. I have no idea why they are still there."

Bishir set about trying to verify that it was *Raleigh News and Observer* editor Jonathan Daniels who had coined the phrase "Unpainted Aristocracy." Daniels sent her a postcard admitting his observation, which to Bishir seemed an ideal description of the place. Bishir chronicled the Nags Head story in an article, "The Unpainted Aristocracy: The Beach Cottages of Old Nags Head," which appeared in the *North Carolina Historical Review* in 1977. (The article was later published separately in a paperback edition.) The designation of the Nags Head Beach Cottage Row Historic District came that same year. The district includes some sixty structures.

Tourists continued coming, their cottage keys changing hands weekly. It seemed to some that all of America had discovered Nags Head. Some vacationers now drove nearly a thousand miles to the Outer Banks, their cars bearing Ohio, New Jersey, and Pennsylvania plates; their journeys often took longer than the boat trip from Elizabeth City that old Nags Headers remembered from a century before. These new Nags Headers came not just to relax on the porch with a book, but to shop at the trendy boutiques, art galleries, and trinket shops dotting the beach road and the bypass.

Though the old Nags Headers still kept to themselves, their summer lives changed, too, as mothers began working, families divorced, and fewer of them stayed the whole summer.

Charlie Reber continued to work on the cottages, but he soon found that this new breed of Nags Header was not to his liking. "I was nailing shingles on a ninety-degree day," he recalls. "I was dry, and I was dusty." On a day like that, says Reber, it was not unusual for the cottage owners to encourage him to help himself to a glass of iced tea or lemonade from the refrigerator. But the new owner of the cottage where he was working had a different view. "He looked up and said he was going out," says Reber, "but if I needed anything to drink, there was a paper cup by the water hose next to the porch. I knew right then it was the beginning of change."

J. Peter Rascoe III sensed the changes, too. He also felt a pull to preserve what his family treasured about Nags Head. While in college in the late 1970s, he visited friends at other beaches. He came away from those visits feeling lucky to have his particular family place. "I didn't sense that they had the same kind of life that we had here [at Nags Head]," he says. "It was always like coming back home. To this day, I

THE FRONT PORCH OF THE RASCOE COTTAGE, BUILT BY J. PETER RASCOE, SR., IN 1931,
SITS ACROSS THE BEACH ROAD FROM JOCKEY'S RIDGE.

Photo by Drew Crawford Wilson

see more family here in the summer than I do at Christmas or Thanksgiving or other holidays."

Fewer families were bringing servants to care for the children during the summer. It was this new generation of Nags Headers who realized—perhaps for the first time—that many in the outside world didn't share or understand their patrician way of life.

"Sometimes, I look at this enclave and it seems so privileged, so willfully turning its back on the real world," says Florence Nash. "I remember when I was a child, our cottage was next to the Arlington Hotel, and you'd hear the clatter of the black staff washing dishes, and they'd walk out to the ocean in white uniforms in the early evening, but they couldn't go in swimming because it was a white beach.

"It was such an innocent, absolute, closed society. I cherish it so much and am so fortunate that I had that kind of background, the privilege of place, knowing you belong because you know everybody else in it, and it was unchanged year after year. But it raised questions that were not easy to answer. When too much is made of the sentiment, a part of me worries over that."

Many of the older servants were aging out. Carleigh Moore, who had worked for the Rascoe family for three generations, died in 1984. "I was at Nags Head when I heard she had died," Peter recalls. "I remember crying. I was so sad. I wondered how it would be without Carleigh."

By then, he was beginning to understand his legacy. He moved to the city for a while, but Nags Head was never far from his thoughts. He later moved to Edenton, where today he is within easy access of the beach. Now the father of two small girls, he finally took his daughters to the top of Jockey's Ridge in the summer of 2000, a walk he made most every day of his childhood at Nags Head.

Having witnessed the sea approaching from the east and development from the north, south, and west, Peter has become more involved in making sure those who visit the area know and understand its value to North Carolina's history. Collecting a history of Nags Head became his passion. He researched his connection to the generations before him who had spent their summers at Nags Head, reading everything he could about the place. A particular treasure is a book by a cousin of his, Captain Edward R. Outlaw, Jr. Called *Old Nags Head*, it documents the early settlement of the resort through family recollections.

Peter has watched the old structures give way to sea and wind, only to be replaced by new cottages that show no relation to Nags Head's distinctive gray-shingled style.

"As a child, I heard stories always connecting the family with the structure. I think that's where my appreciation started," he says. "Nowadays, people come and stay in a condo or a house on the sound, and you don't identify them with the place. As time went on, I visited other places and saw how maybe they were like this at one time, but how development took off, and a lot of these structures disappeared. I became more interested in learning more about the structures

PETER RASCOE III AND HIS DAUGHTERS LUCY MAE AND KATIE TAKE A MORNING STROLL TO THE BEACH.

Photo by Drew Crawford Wilson

and the history behind them and what really drew people here. It was always that these were the families they were kin to, and it was the style of the cottages. So much of the history of the development was centered around who built them, where they were built, and it was so interesting to me. . . . I have a deep sense of trying to hold on to something I feel strongly about.

"My two brothers feel the same way I do, a sense that we all want to be here. As long as the same families come back, I'll have that feeling. If a storm wiped it all out, I'd try to hang on to it. When I moved back here, I thought, 'Why do I have it so deep?' I'm never leaving again."

In recent years, Peter has been involved in planning seasonal tours of the old cottages, opening them up to hundreds of visitors for the first time. At first, the families were reluctant, unsure of the notoriety the tours would bring.

"I sat down with every single family who owned a piece of any cottage—and sometimes that's four and five families for one house—and I sat down with them in their living rooms. It took six months to plan the first tour."

When he is at Nags Head, he walks the beach constantly with his two daughters, introducing them to their distant cousins, collecting shells, building sand castles.

"They can't wander the dunes while their parents take naps like we used to do, but I try to make sure they know the same families. One thing that is the same is that we stay in touch constantly. I know of nobody who comes down here and locks themselves up in their house and watches television all week."

"People say Nags Head has changed so much," says Nancy Rascoe. "But at our part of the beach, it's the same people, the second and third generations. That really hasn't changed. I hope so much to be able to keep Nags Head. I feel more strongly about handing that down than anything."

"We are just regular folks who have an ingrained desire to be together," says Peter. "To some, that might come across as standoffish. But a lot of people who come to the Outer Banks have no appreciation for the history of this place. I remember as a kid wondering, 'Will it all be there when we come back?' So far, it's been here every time."

Nags Head remains central to his life. He still packs up his young family at the first of the summer and moves them to the beach. Now, they live on the sound side in a cottage he and his wife own. Though the house his grandfather built is rented some weeks during the summer, Peter joins his family in the oceanfront house in late July.

"Though my parents are older, there is still a sense that we all want to be here," he says. "Now, I want my telephone and my television. But as long as the same families come back during the summer, I'll always want to be here. If you took that strip away, I can see myself going other places in the summer, but I doubt I'd ever feel at home."

BUOYS ON THE RASCOE PORCH
Photo by Drew Crawford Wilson

The Original Nags Header.
Nags Head's Giant Dune

THE WIND CONSTANTLY SHIFTS THE SAND ON JOCKEY'S RIDGE. NO DATE WAS GIVEN ON WHEN THIS PHOTOGRAPH WAS TAKEN.
Courtesy of the North Carolina Collection, University of North Carolina Library at Chapel Hill

The sweeping skirts of Jockey's Ridge—perched between the Atlantic Ocean and the Roanoke Sound—have drawn explorers for centuries.

Perhaps it is the original Nags Header, this giant dune that is the centerpiece of Nags Head. True to the spirit of all Nags Headers, it has constantly reshaped itself, adapting to wind and sand and sea as it overlooks the roofs of the Unpainted Aristocracy.

The tallest active dune on the East Coast, Jockey's Ridge is in fact the largest of a series of naturally formed dunes reaching from Nags Head north to False Cape, Virginia. The 10 million cubic yards of sand that form "the Ridge" are continually shaped by the Outer Banks' prevailing winds—from the northeast for most of the year, shifting southeast during the summer.

Geologists think the sand that first shaped Jockey's Ridge originated in the old Roanoke River inlet system, which existed north of Colington Island eight thousand to ten thousand years ago. The Jockey's Ridge system most likely formed when smaller piles of the inlet's

NOTED NORTH CAROLINA PHOTOGRAPHER BAYARD WOOTTEN CAPTURED THIS SHOT OF JOCKEY'S RIDGE IN THE 1930S.
AN OLD COTTAGE STANDS IN THE BACKGROUND.
Courtesy of the North Carolina Collection, University of North Carolina Library at Chapel Hill

massive sand supply were pinned against the more stable land in the Roanoke River Valley. Though the dune's age is uncertain, recent studies conducted by the North Carolina Department of Environment and Natural Resources show that Jockey's Ridge was formed in layers and may be over eight thousand years old.

From its earliest discovery, people have been flocking to the dune for adventure and a bird's-eye view of the beach. Through the years, the wind has marched the sand back toward the sound, reshaping the dune.

For as long as anyone can remember, Jockey's Ridge has been made up of two dunes, the larger of which stretches over a mile along the island. Jockey's Ridge was once the largest among a group of neighboring dunes, most of which have disappeared through the years but live in the memory of old-time Nags Headers. Round-About Hill, Scraggly Oak Hill, and Graveyard Hill stretched north of Jockey's Ridge, while Engagement Hill, Pin Hill, and the Seven Sisters extended south.

Few who pass the giant dune can resist the urge to climb it. Long before an asphalt road bordered Jockey's Ridge, children from the Unpainted Aristocracy explored all sides of the dune from dawn until dusk. With the advent of the road, travelers could park their cars at the base of the dune and walk up from there. Kids scrambled up the first hill, then tumbled back down. Most can recall falling into the unexplored territory on the back side of the Ridge.

Though it was private property for many years,

Jockey's Ridge has always been considered public domain. From Nags Head's earliest days, the dune drew tourists like a magnet, and its owners made no attempt to curb visitation. Today, close to nine hundred thousand visitors climb the dune each year, including thirteen thousand hang gliders, who take flight from its peak.

The Ridge has long been fodder for local lore.

Blackbeard is said to have buried a chest full of gold on the seaward side of the dune, his pirate band marching across the sand from the *Queen Anne's Revenge*, which was anchored in the Roanoke Sound. According to legend, a Banker who witnessed the burial was killed on the spot, so as not to reveal the site of the treasure. That may have been unwise on Blackbeard's part. When the pirates returned to retrieve their treasure, the wind had shifted the sand, so the chest was lost. Some say that the ghostly shapes of Blackbeard's men can still be seen traipsing over the dune in search of the elusive gold.

The dune was also a favorite site for Nags Headers to court. Legend says that taking an unmarried lady to the summit would soon make her your wife.

Jockey's Ridge is the subject of wartime tales as well. It was used as a navigational aid by French and Spanish sailors in the 1700s. Some say that during World War II, local spies would climb to the summit on dark nights and signal to the U-boats lingering offshore. And many Nags Headers claim that the upstart fighter pilots known as the Black Sheep Squadron, who trained in Manteo for a time, aimed at Jockey's Ridge on their way to an official bombing range farther north in Duck. The dune in fact was used for aerial gunnery practice by the

SKIING DOWN JOCKEY'S RIDGE, C. 1950
IN THE BACKGROUND ARE THE NAGS HEAD CASINO AND THE UNPAINTED ARISTOCRACY.
Courtesy of the Outer Banks History Center

navy during World War II (and is now named on the official cleanup list of former defense sites by the United States Department of Defense). Later in the war, Jeep races along the back side of the dune were a favorite sport.

Many visitors to the Ridge don't realize that it is a living, breathing being home to two rare plant species—woolly beach heather and maritime pinweed—as well as dozens of species of animals.

In the early 1970s, as Nags Head's growth began to mushroom, word came to locals that a development company wanted to construct condominiums on the northwest edge of Jockey's Ridge. In 1973, locals led by

Carolista Fletcher Baum Golden launched a movement to establish the dune as a state park. Though many expressed concern that a state park would ruin the dune, the state authorized $500,000 to acquire the land. On June 7, 1975, the state established the 414-acre Jockey's Ridge State Park to protect the dune's unique geologic formation from development and stabilization. The dune system is now a National Natural Landmark and a North Carolina Natural Heritage Area.

Though the Outer Banks' ecosystems have been studied for years, the Jockey's Ridge site has come under scientific scrutiny only recently. For many years, it was thought that the sheer size of the dune would protect it from changes brought about by the area's growth.

In 1996, the North Carolina Division of Environment and Natural Resources began conducting a study of Jockey's Ridge. The state discovered that the dune system's sand supply had diminished through time, and that local wind patterns may well have been affected by the growth of buildings in the area of the dune. According to Marshall Ellis, resource management specialist with the North Carolina Division of Parks and Recreation, more recent research indicates that the dune system is "sediment starved." In other words, it was formed as the result of rare geological events in an area that has never received vast amounts of replenishing sand. "The bottom line is that there isn't enough loose sand in the immediate neighborhood to guarantee the long-term care and feeding of a giant like Jockey's Ridge," says Ellis. "It's a long, slow path toward eventually spreading out over the landscape. Over the last century, steady losses occurred long before development

boomed, and those losses have been one of the few ecological constants."

Like an aging lady who begins to stoop with time, the Ridge has lost its height in recent years. In 1900, it stood 140 feet above sea level, reaching its maximum height in late winter. Measurements in more recent years have marked the height at 110.5 feet in 1974, 107 feet in 1979, 99.4 feet in 1993, and 87 feet today. Recent high-tech 3-D studies of the dune's volume show that, though elevation loss is dramatic, 99 percent of the dune system's sand is still inside the park area. The smaller dune has shifted 400 feet south since 1974, while the larger dune's ridge and summit have drifted around 200 feet.

Despite its shifting sands, Jockey's Ridge isn't likely to disappear in the next century. But like the Unpainted Aristocracy it watches over, Jockey's Ridge fights its own battles against age, growth, and the sea.

THE UNPAINTED ARISTOCRACY AS SEEN FROM JOCKEY'S RIDGE TODAY
Photo by Drew Crawford Wilson

"Carleigh was just as much a part of our Nags Head summers as anything."
Carleigh Speller Moore

CARLEIGH SPELLER MOORE HOLDS THE INFANT PETER RASCOE III, IN AUGUST 1957.
Courtesy of J. Peter Rascoe III

The servants who helped care for Nags Head's children often spent years with families, caring for one generation after the other. J. Peter Rascoe III recalls his family's cook and nursemaid, Carleigh Speller Moore, who, by the time Rascoe was a boy, had worked for the family for nearly fifty years. Each summer, she traveled with the Rascoes to Nags Head, where she stayed in the maid's quarters in back of Peter's grandfather's cottage.

Carleigh was a descendant of slaves. She was born and raised on the Speller Farm in Bertie County. She later moved to Elizabeth City. She worked for my grandmother Edna Jones Nixon Dawson in Elizabeth City and helped raise my mother and her sister and brother. She spent most every summer at Nags Head with them when they were growing up. Later, after my parents were mar-

ried, Carleigh helped my mother every summer at the Rascoe Cottage, staying in a room in the detached garage, a typical maid's quarters for Nags Head beach cottages. She had two small beds, a toilet, and sink all in the same room. For years, she used the same suitcase. Her wire glasses always sat on top of her Bible. Her porch had benches built in, too, just like the main cottage. We called it "Carleigh's house."

Carleigh raised my two younger brothers and me during our summers at Nags Head. We still have a picture of her in a rocking chair on the porch holding me the summer I was born. As we grew, Carleigh was in charge of us most every day as my mother tried to enjoy her time at Nags Head. In those early days, we moved down for the whole summer. My father would come on weekends from Windsor after farming all week.

Carleigh was just as much a part of our Nags Head summers as anything I can think of. She would cook three meals a day, wash clothes in the Rascoe Cottage's old tub washing machine with its roller wringers, and spend the days keeping an eye on us as we played out in the sand. Many mornings, I remember her sitting with us in the dunes in the yard, showing us how to scoop sand with a shell. I remember her in a green cotton dress with the biggest apron I have ever seen.

She loved to walk barefoot but always had her worn, classic foam flip-flops close by. Sometimes, she would walk us to the beach, but only to let us put our feet in the wash, since she couldn't swim. Carleigh even took us up on Jockey's Ridge when we were young. I remember a few times her climbing to the top with us. She would come from the side, not straight up like we did. We could see her with that apron flying in the wind at the bottom, and we knew it was her. There were flats there that would flood. She would walk through the water with us. We used to sail homemade sailboats in those ponds. Sometimes, she would wait at the base for us to climb the rest of the way up and roll back down. I can't imagine my child walking across that street without anybody now.

At nap time and at night, she would tell us stories about growing up as a young girl in Bertie County. She used to talk about coming to town on Saturdays, when she used to go to the Rascoe Store, which was a typical farm commissary. She told us about picking cotton as a child and stacking peanuts. She was very proud of the fact that she was a Speller, that she had family back in Bertie. Her son was a master sergeant in the service in Turkey.

Many of Carleigh's friends from Elizabeth City worked in the old cottages. Sometimes, she would take off to visit them. One time as a child, I cut two fingers whittling. They were bad cuts, and my parents were gone somewhere. Carleigh was very nervous. My fingers were spouting blood. She grabbed them and squeezed my hand and pulled me right across the yards to see her friend Rena at Janie Outlaw Flora's cottage. I remember Rena helped her tend my cuts and then told Carleigh to take me back home and read to me.

As the years went by, we became more rambunctious and more of a challenge for Carleigh to handle. Many times, we would hear her say, "Where is my fly swat?" when we misbehaved or walked into her kitchen with wet and sandy feet. "How awful," she would say to let us know she didn't approve of something she saw us say or do. That included my parents and grandparents.

Carleigh didn't drive. She always rode the Trailways bus. In the 1960s and '70s, there was scheduled bus service on the beach to Elizabeth City. You could stand out in front of the cottage on the beach road and flag the bus down. On summer days, if Carleigh had business in Elizabeth City, she would ride the bus back to town. Sometimes, we rode with her for the day. It was the first time I'd ever ridden a bus. It was full of whites and blacks. There was no back-seat-of-the-bus stuff. I sat right by her. She knew how to flag one down and to pull the cord to get off. Whenever we were riding in the car with our parents and saw a Trailways bus, we would say, "There's Carleigh!" Carleigh would sometimes come to Windsor on the bus during the year to help my mother. It was like a special reminder that the daily routine at the beach was sure to follow.

Back then, there was of course no television and no local radio stations at Nags Head, but some AM radio stations could be picked up at night. We read about approaching storms in the newspapers. Carleigh was scared of hurricanes—so scared that the minute she heard there was a hurricane anywhere in the Atlantic Ocean, she would pack up and leave Nags Head on the bus. My mother tried not to talk about the weather around Carleigh. Sometimes, bad storms would sneak up on her,

and so she was doubtful of my mother being forthcoming about approaching weather. Sometimes, when my mother and father were entertaining their Nags Head friends, Wood Beasley of Colerain would tease Carleigh, telling her there was a hurricane on the way. I remember several times she left us on the next day's bus.

When Carleigh was riding with us in the car, she never liked to cross the big bridges. She would always flip that big apron over her head until we safely came to the other side.

Of course, as the years went by, she moved slower and slower. She kept her "fly swat" handy, though. Even though we'd grown older and didn't need watching anymore, Carleigh still came to Nags Head to stay with us at the Rascoe Cottage or with my Dawson grandparents at their cottage. For about ten years, she didn't stay in the maid's quarters, but in the main cottage. I'd look at the sand dune in the side yard and remember her sitting there, her legs stretched out, scooping up sand for sand castles. When we put a new washer and dryer in the cottage, I knew Carleigh's time was gone.

Carleigh died in June of 1984. Everybody congregated at her house in Elizabeth City. Three generations of our family attended her funeral, sitting up front in the church with Carleigh's family. I still remember very clearly that day looking down at Carleigh in the open casket and thinking that if I ever had children, they would probably never have anyone like Carleigh. We loved Carleigh, and I know she loved us. I still think of her every summer at Nags Head.

Riptide

WHAT REMAINS OF THE UNPAINTED ARISTOCRACY ALONG NAGS HEAD'S COTTAGE ROW
FROM LEFT: THE FRANK WOOD COTTAGE, 1923; THE FRED P. WOOD COTTAGE, 1935;
THE PRUDEN-BATTLE-CLARK COTTAGE, 1915; THE WOOD-FOREMAN COTTAGE, 1916;
AND THE MACMULLAN COTTAGE, 1866.

Photo by Drew Crawford Wilson

> Riptide, n. A commotion of the sea caused by opposing currents or by a rapid current passing over an uneven bottom; to carry, as the tide does.
>
> *The Oxford*
> *English Dictionary*

V. RIPTIDE: SWIRLING INTO THE NEW CENTURY, 1990-

THE NAGS HEAD OF MEMORY is all but gone. These days, just north of the Nags Head city limits, N.C. 158 Bypass is littered with pizza parlors, New York-style delis, and shops that sell everything from boogie boards to toothpaste. Up the road in Kill Devil Hills, shoppers jam the K-mart in search of bargains, almost within view of the spot where the Wright brothers made their famous flight. And the aisles at Wal-Mart in Kitty Hawk are often more crowded than the fishing pier when the blues are running. Just south of the Unpainted Aristocracy, shoppers flock to the outlet mall on rainy days.

Traffic jams are common from June to August, when Nags Head's population swells from two thousand to forty thousand, a new crop of tourists moving in each week. Today's vacationers seem to spend more time driving than they do enjoying sand and water.

Summer residents of the old cottages rarely venture north toward Duck and trendy Corolla to see the marks the new Outer Banks vacationers have left on the beach. Pastel dream homes with leaded-glass front doors facing the street line the oceanfront. They bear little resemblance to the ramshackle cottages twenty miles south, whose front porches were designed a century ago to catch the ocean breeze.

Possum Silver took part in the building boom on the barrier island in the last part of the twentieth century. As a building contractor, he constructed cottages along the entire Outer Banks from Avon to

LIGHT SIFTS THROUGH THE WINDOWS OF THE BUCHANAN DINING ROOM.

Photo by Drew Crawford Wilson

Corolla, from three-bedroom beach boxes to four-thousand-square-foot dream homes with hot tubs and gourmet kitchens.

"These developers came in here and said, 'We've got to make it like Charleston or Key West,'" Silver recalls. "I told them, 'What's wrong with making it look like Old Nags Head?'"

While many of the structures that comprise the Unpainted Aristocracy have remained much as they were at the turn of the twentieth century, descendants of the families who helped establish Nags Head have embraced the twenty-first century in different

ways. The Buchanans have established a limited partnership to manage and maintain their family cottage, now shared by over twenty-five people of three generations. Though it was never rented in its early days, the cottage now rents for portions of the summer. Randy Coupland's mother died several years ago, leaving him and his brother her inheritance in the house, which he now shares with his aunts, Mary Frances Flowers and Anne Tomlinson. Two other sisters have been bought out by the remaining three families.

The old cottage continues to hold its sense of mystery for a new generation of Buchanans, who often congregate on the same front porch where Coupland's grandfather shared a conversation with the president more than half a century ago.

"When I first saw it, I thought it was a huge place," says Coupland's stepson, Wesley Lyon, who first visited the house when he was around ten years old. "It was a little creepy, a little scary, because it was old, and the wind from the ocean blows through it. The wind is everywhere. I don't really like the upstairs by myself, even when it's summer."

For Wesley, the history of the house was brought to life one chilly Easter weekend when he and his friend Matt Rollins of Raleigh went to Nags Head with the Coupland family.

"I remember it was real cold and windy," Wesley recalls. "I was sleeping in a different room, because the room I always stayed in was occupied. I was sleeping in shorts, and I was cold, so I got up and put on long pants and a jacket, but I was still cold. I looked up at the ceiling, then looked straight ahead of me, and I saw this man. He was bald, and he looked crippled, and he was writing at a desk. He kept writing and writing. My heart was beating so fast. I thought I should get up, but I was shaking, and my friend was fast asleep. I must have looked at him for about five minutes. Then I looked away and back at him, but he was gone."

When Wesley, who says he didn't sleep at all the rest of the night, told his parents the next morning, his stepfather was not surprised. "I knew you'd see him," said Coupland. "That was my grandfather."

Wesley had slept in John Adams Buchanan's room.

"I never thought anything like that was true before," says Wesley. "I've thought about it a lot since then, about what he might have been writing. I think he was writing his will, about who the house goes to. I never really believed in ghosts, but now I'm not so sure. Maybe I was meant to see him, and maybe I'll see him again. It's not a scary thing to me anymore; it's a special thing."

Wesley says he didn't know much about the history of the cottage when he first visited, except the story of President Roosevelt. Now, he is intrigued. "I'm thinking there are secret passageways through the cracks in the wall," he says. "I want to go exploring through it now."

Perhaps it is the link among the generations within the houses that Nags Headers treasure the most.

Unlike so many of the vacationers who surround them, the families of Old Nags Head come not to scavenge strip malls and trendy beach shops, but to dive into a wave, catch a fish, find a shell, share a meal, and tell a tale about life before the tourists came. Though tourists pass the Unpainted Aristocracy by the thousands on any summer day, they may not realize the lives the cottagers live sequestered from newcomers. It is a life grand in its simplicity.

"The people who live in these cottages are just like we are," says Anne Buchanan Tomlinson. "We are just there. It is a stretch of family beach, that mile. It's still going on. We didn't have a telephone until

THE PATINA OF THE KITCHEN POTS GIVES EVIDENCE OF THEIR YEARS OF USE AS THEY SIT STACKED ON THE SHELVES IN THE BUCHANAN KITCHEN.

Photo by Drew Crawford Wilson

about fifteen years ago, and no television until three years ago. My children grew up, and their children are growing up now, loving just being here. They all fish, they all swim, having a grand time playing under the house. It's amazing that out of all of them, everybody loves the beach."

The love of beach remains, though the cottages may not. Four of the original thirteen Nags Head cottages are gone. The Drane Cottage, where Jaquelin Nash spent her childhood summers, was moved to a narrow sand hill at the base of Jockey's Ridge after

the Ash Wednesday Storm in 1962. Artists captured it—its sunken roof dripping with kudzu vines—in watercolors and photographs for close to forty years. Then, in the spring of 2000, despite efforts by Preservation North Carolina to find a buyer, the old place was razed, its weathered wood hauled away.

But the Drane descendants still hold fast to their Nags Head roots.

"People say to me, 'Why Nags Head? It has golf courses and smells like old frying grease,' " says Florence Nash, who grew up in Tarboro and has lived in Durham for many years. Despite the fact that the house she shared with her family all those years ago no longer exists, her love for Nags Head has never wavered.

"You can't translate rationally the depth of feeling I have for something that no longer exists physically," she says. "That cottage was more of an ancestral center for me than our inland house. We always heard stories of my mother and her cousins when they were little, so there was a very potent sense of taking part in a continuum, being surrounded by family, both living and dead.

"In a way, your passages are sometimes set in your mind in physical places. When I think about continuity of family and am aware of being part of multiple generations, I think about that house, because that's where we were with cousins we didn't see all the time, grandparents who were always there, and because so many family stories were centered there. There is not a match for anything else in my life. I did so much of my growing up there. We were so much in the presence of family, and they were so happy. People's lives were not easy, but they were so happy at Nags Head. We got the benefit of their teaching at their emotional best.

"People felt so free, and that is the legacy. They were happy because it was a family house and because they had wonderful memories. The potent thing is a state of mind."

Despite the loss of some of the structures, most Nags Headers will attest that it is the roots that matter most. Possum Silver is afraid that his generation will be the last to really understand how deeply Nags Headers are linked by those roots.

"My kids won't have that," says Silver. "We're the last ones. We had the best of it. We never had any money, but we had that place, and we knew it. We had all the connections, the old way of life. We try to hold on to it for our kids, but they won't have that connection."

Silver has seen his sleepy stretch of beach transformed into a busy thoroughfare with too many stoplights and a bypass filled with vacationers. They help themselves to what's not theirs, he says, making the beach unsafe for his three children to roam like he did as a kid.

"One day, my son, who was seven, asked me if I'd ever been fishing on a pier. I can remember going to the pier with a bucket and a pole when I was seven years old and spending the whole night," he recalls. "I'd never let him do that now, because there are too many people down here now without any home training."

These newcomers have changed Possum Silver's Nags Head forever. "They come here because they love it," he says. "Then they want to make it 'where I came from.' "

It was this "where I came from" attitude that prompted Silver to toss his hammer into the discard pile and begin a new career a few years ago as an artist. Now, he saves with watercolors what developers didn't want him to build. "I can draw anything that light shines on," he says. His work, which he signs with his given name of John Silver, is a study of color, shadow, and light. Images of the old cottages, of fishermen who comb the sea for their livelihood, of children squatting to collect treasured shells—all are impressions of the Nags Head that Silver clings to. One watercolor, of a lone cottage against a barren landscape, bears the title *The Way It Used to Be.*

Change is everywhere. No longer do just a handful of families pile into St. Andrew's-by-the-Sea during the summer months. Today, the Episcopal sanctuary, still its original size, is filled to overflowing each Sunday throughout the year; parishioners often spill out into the parking lot on holidays. A new Episcopal parish has been established north of Nags Head in Kitty Hawk to accommodate the growth of year-round Outer Banks residents, and a new St. Andrew's sanctuary will soon be built next to the old church. The original 1915 S. J. Twine structure will be preserved.

ST. ANDREW'S-BY-THE-SEA AS IT LOOKS TODAY

Photo by Drew Crawford Wilson

ABOVE LEFT: THE FRONT
DOOR THAT LEADS INTO THE
SMALL CHAPEL HONORS
MARIAN DRANE GRAHAM.
ABOVE RIGHT: THE ORIGINAL
PEWS OF ST. ANDREW'S-BY-
THE-SEA, LEFT: VIEW FROM
THE LOFT OF ST. ANDREW'S-
BY-THE-SEA

Photos by Drew Crawford Wilson

The families of Nags Head understand how important their cottages are not only to them, but to the history of North Carolina and the Outer Banks. They are committed to preserving their legacy as long as the sea allows.

"These old cottages have a seemingly contradictory quality that captures the imagination," says Catherine Bishir, who conducted the research for the historic district in 1977. "They epitomize a traditional view among the old aristocracy of North Carolina that you don't have to show off to know who you are. These folks are mighty proud of not being proud. [It's] not at all like the new ostentatiousness that surrounds them.

"This is so much a North Carolina attitude," she says. "I hate to see it disappear. These families have chosen to hang on to these special places, and that is extraordinary. With the big, horrible beach palaces all around them, these modest, unpretentious ones become more of a treasure."

☙

In February 1998, the series of northeasters that brushed the coast tore the roof off Possum Silver's mother's cottage, taking with it fifty feet of beach in front of where the house stood. There was no question that the cottage would be moved and repaired, as it had been at least three times in its life, which has entered its third century.

The night of one of the storms, Silver worked to save the house as if it were a living, breathing member of his family. He summoned his brother Winkie,

who lives in nearby Wanchese, and the two worked until dawn to shore up the house from underneath, braving weather so cold it stiffened their hands.

As the winds calmed and spring set in, Silver went to work rebuilding, repairing, and restoring the aristocratic lady who had drawn his family to her aproned porches since the eighteenth century.

"This house was only here by habit," says Silver, who after the storms took the cottage apart, only to find that a century of seawater and salt air had caused most of the nails to disintegrate. Though he replaced the maid's quarters with a new wing across the back of the house complete with air conditioning, heat, and a full bath, the rest of the cottage remains as it has been since anyone can remember.

Betty Howison was the first old-time Nags Header to take advantage of a recent law allowing property owners to use part of the money spent on renovating a historic house as credit on state income taxes. With the help of the North Carolina Historic Preservation Office, Silver wrote a history of the cottage and designed a restoration plan that followed preservation guidelines.

Nags Headers like Silver wonder if the thousands of tourists who pass by Cottage Row every summer can fully appreciate the history, the simplicity of the life seeping deep into the juniper shingles.

Yet no matter how much these families hope to clasp tradition, it is the sea that will make the final call. The 1998 move will be the last for the Winston-Wales Cottage. Next time, says Silver, the sea will

A BOWL OF SHELLS SITS IN THE MIDDLE OF THE TABLE IN THE WINSTON-WALES COTTAGE.

Photo by Drew Crawford Wilson

IN THE WINSTON-WALES COTTAGE, A ROPE IS USED TO KEEP THE CURTAIN FROM BLOWING IN THE BREEZE.

Photo by Drew Crawford Wilson

just have to take what it does, legacy or not. The cottage has survived over 125 years of sand and sea, and Silver has done what he can to see that his mother's house lives at least a few years more. But he continues to watch the sea.

"These houses have their own spirit," says Silver, who settled in Manteo some years ago and now owns an art gallery near the waterfront. "I wouldn't try to replicate it. It's in the wood, when you walk in and the floors creak and the paint pops, the windows won't go up or down. If something happened to it, they wouldn't let you build it back like that. You can build a new house with a covered porch, but it wouldn't be the same. It's like when the spirit leaves the body.

"Everybody assumes that they are grand, but if they go inside, they're floored by how simple they are. There is a mystery about them. The name Unpainted Aristocracy suits it, or maybe Arrogantly Shabby would be better. There is an air about them, the air of the Southern aristocrat. The folks who live in them are connected by that spirit; we all have it, and we can never replace it if it's lost."

"It's like a death in the family."
The Death of an Old House, the Birth of the New

THE NIXON COTTAGE, BUILT IN 1866, SURVIVED 134 YEARS OF HURRICANES AND NORTHEASTERS BEFORE IT WAS RAZED IN 2000. IT WAS REPLACED IN 2001 BY A REPLICA—THE SAME SIZE AND DESIGN AS THE ORIGINAL.
Photo by Drew Crawford Wilson

The old Nixon Cottage had a soul. The dining-room floor sagged each time anyone walked on it. The porch eaves were covered with residue from over a hundred Nags Head winters.

Perhaps the Nixon Cottage symbolizes the drama that may one day play out among all the cottages of the Unpainted Aristocracy. Built as a four-room fishing shack by Florence Grandy in 1866 and sold to Thomas Nixon, Dee Read's grandfather, in 1908, the cottage was remodeled many times by S. J. Twine. Twine even added a second story to accommodate the growing Nixon family.

The cottage was quintessential Nags Head. Louvered doors separated the bedrooms for the easy circulation of sea air. Wide roofs sheltered the wraparound porches from rain. Wooden spools doubled as cabinet handles. Seashells hung by strings from the overhead lights. There was no indoor shower.

It survived hurricanes in 1899 and 1933, and again in 1999, when mildew left behind by Hurricanes Dennis and Floyd stained the ceiling in the northeast bedroom upstairs. Northeasters were too many to count, like the Ash Wednesday Storm, when sand filled the porches to the ceiling.

But as its third century approached, the family knew there were no more battles left in the old house.

Troubled by the approaching Atlantic, Dee Read of Hertford and her cousin Lloyd Horton of Florida knew the house—one of the original thirteen that had stood at Nags Head's oceanfront since the 1850s—would have to be moved. The cousins called in engineers and historic preservationists, who one by one determined the cottage could not be moved and still hold together.

Read did not let go of her beloved beach home easily. She combed the old house before its demolition, marking pieces that could be salvaged to make the new seem old. The hand-wrought banister and newel posts from the original staircase would be added to a new staircase, which would be widened to meet building-code specifications. The upstairs three-quarter-inch heart-pine floors would be remilled, to be recast as downstairs flooring. An overhead beam from the kitchen was also deemed usable, as were the shutters and an old wooden table on the back porch.

The Nixon Cottage had weathered 134 years of wind, sand, and rain and had been moved many times. But in the fall of 2000, the house was razed.

As bulldozers made their first pass into the seven-bedroom house, the walls collapsed into the sand like a deck of cards. But within weeks, a new cottage sprang up in its place, its rust-colored, shingled frame standing in stark contrast to the soft gray lines of the existing cottage line. For a passerby, the shingles might serve as the only distinction between the old Nixon and the new,

since the new cottage is a replica of the original, from its L shape to its wraparound porches to its protruding benches.

Just before it was torn down, Read made her last visit to stay in the old house. While there, she reflected on the loss of the only place she ever really thought of as home, and on how she would adjust the first time she entered the new Nixon Cottage.

When my grandfather bought this place, it was one floor, four rooms. Mr. Twine added the second floor. In the old days, everything was painted with a white trim.

Emma Rouse was our cook. I came down with mother's twin sister the summer of 1929 and spent the whole summer because Mother was expecting my sister. The house wasn't built up very high then.

It has taken me a year, but I've resigned myself to the fact that it can't be saved. There is nothing left to nail to. A strong wind would come and lift the whole roof up. The rustic way you did things down here that are not very convenient, [like] washing clothes in a washtub, why would I miss that?

My children always said coming here was always like coming home. We moved around so much, every two or three years. It's my seventy-third summer at Nags Head. I will miss the history. It's like a death in the family. I think losing it hits me harder than most.

In the old cottage, there is no indoor shower, only one shower on the back porch. The new cottage will have two dishwashers, bathtubs. It will be computer-friendly.

It will be the same floor plan, seven bedrooms. The windows and porches will be in the same place.

My grandfather fixed a side porch to be twelve feet wide, with no gaps in the boards, so his daughters could have dances out here with an old-fashioned wind-up Victrola.

My father invented a type of hinge made out of two blocks of teak and a large brass pin set into it to separate the two blocks. The contractor was so carried away with it when he found it that he's having them copied to put on the outside shutters. When he removed the old pilings, he found a concrete driveway six feet under the sand.

We'll salvage what we can, [like] the stair rail and banister. Most of the furniture is old, but we're going to refinish it and put it back. The dining-room furniture was made from trees that fell down at our farm in Hertford during a hurricane. We will have air conditioning and heat, which we don't have now. But I don't have to use it. We've even considered heating the back bedroom in case somebody wants to come down during the winter.

On my last trip, we were so busy we worked from dawn till bedtime packing up. Everything we picked up was some sort of memory. I had some misgivings. That last day, I dragged my heels. My cousin's wife, Carolyn, and I did it alone. She said, "Are you ready? I think you're not quite ready. You want to be alone." So she let me go in alone.

I walked through every room, remembering every

DEE READ'S PARENTS, MARJORY NIXON OAKEY AND WALTER OAKEY, SHARE A MOMENT ON THE FRONT STEPS OF THE NIXON COTTAGE IN THE 1920S.
Photo courtesy of Dee Read

DEE READ (SECOND FROM LEFT) AND SEVERAL MEMBERS OF HER FAMILY SIT IN FRONT OF (PICTURED IN BACKGROUND FROM LEFT TO RIGHT) THE NIXON COTTAGE, THE BADHAM-KITTRELL COTTAGE, AND THE BUCHANAN COTTAGE.
Photo courtesy of Dee Read

association for seventy-three years. When I walked through the kitchen, I remembered seeing biscuits come out of the wood stove. I can see my grandmother right now, making boiled pudding with peaches or blackberries and butter and sugar. She would roll it up and pinch it inside of a crust. Then she'd sew it up in a piece of white cloth like a bedsheet and drop it in a pot of boiling water. "Taste that and see if we need more seasoning," she was always saying to me. She used to sit on the back porch and eat those parched peanuts, blowing the hulls off into the wind. We'd watch the fishermen bring in their nets early in the morning, and the servants would go out and choose some fish, then we'd have fish and grits for breakfast. A lot of my memories are not all mine. It's what my grandmother and mother told me.

When I was a teenager, I was locked out a few times and would climb through the window. There was one step on the stairs I'd have to be careful with because it squeaked. We all sat down in the dining room three times a day at the right time; there was no grab something and run. We used to go up and down the beach, all over the place, my sister and I when we were seven or eight years old. Now, you can't let your grandchildren walk down the beach alone.

I said good-bye to the house just like you would for someone who was passing away. When I saw it after everything salvageable had been taken out, it was nothing but a shell. None of the past generations had ever seen it like that, not in five generations. I cried when I drove off.

FROM LEFT: COUSINS MOLLY OAKEY BRODIE, NANCY DAWSON RASCOE, AND DEE OAKEY READ STAND ON THE BACK STEPS OF THE NIXON COTTAGE IN 1941.
Photo courtesy of Dee Read

The new cottage will be a rebirth and a replica. I hope it will be a place to create memories, until the ocean takes it. The last time I came down, I stayed at the Nags Head Inn, and I avoided going by it. But when I did go, there was nothing there. This house is gone, just gone.

My half of the cottage will go to my four children. I hope it will be passed down. The new house will still be on the same spot. I'll do everything I can to make it feel like the old house. I hope it will feel the same with the old furniture.

Everybody wants to move into the twenty-first century, but they don't have the memories I do.

THE NIXON COTTAGE, SPRING 2001

THE ORIGINAL COTTAGE, BUILT IN 1866, WAS RAZED IN 2000 AND REPLACED WITH ONE SIMILAR IN ARCHITECTURE, BUT WITH
MODERN AMENITIES LIKE CENTRAL HEAT AND AIR CONDITIONING. THE BANISTER, UPSTAIRS FLOORBOARDS, AND SHUTTERS WERE
SALVAGED AND USED IN THE NEW COTTAGE, ENSURING THAT IT RETAINED ITS OLD NAGS HEAD CHARACTER.

Photo by Drew Crawford Wilson

THE FRANK WINSLOW COTTAGE, ALSO KNOWN AS WINDEMERE, CASTS A SHADOW AGAINST
THE SUNSET. THE HOUSE WAS BUILT BY S. J. TWINE AROUND 1934.

Photo by Drew Crawford Wilson

EPILOGUE

*I*N THE END, it is about belonging. We are defined by a memory, a house, a place, our lives set in motion because of where we were first known for who we are.

Nags Head is just such a place, and the memory of it pulls people to it like the tides. They come year after year, generation upon next, prying open faded shutters, opening windows, welcoming the salt air. They come in the shadow of those who swept the porch before them, imagining those who'll join the continuum after they're gone. It is that sense of family and that history—a plain house with juniper shingles, a wide porch that shelters from the rain, curtains billowed out by a sea breeze—that make them love the place, draw them to it.

And though they have kept it now for over a hundred years, the survival of the Unpainted Aristocracy may no longer be in the hands of those who love it most. The irony may be that the tides that first drew Nags Headers may also make the final call.

A HAMMOCK PROVIDES THE PERFECT PLACE TO RELAX ON THE BUCHANAN FAMILY PORCH.

Photo by Drew Crawford Wilson

APPENDIX 1: INTERVIEWS CONDUCTED BY THE AUTHOR

Bishir, Catherine. Raleigh, N.C., 5 December 2000.

Coupland, Randy. Raleigh, N.C., 14 January 2000 and 21 April 2000.

Crawford, Betty. Nags Head, N.C., 3 August 1998.

Deal, Bill. Virginia Beach, Va., 16 September 2000.

Ellis, Marshall. Raleigh, N.C., November 2000.

Fearing, Fred. Elizabeth City, N.C., 20 April 2000.

Ferguson, Gary. Nags Head, N.C., 3 August 1998.

Flowers, Mary Frances. Richmond, Va., November 1999; Raleigh, N.C., 15 January 2000.

Gill, Charles. Nags Head, N.C., 4 August 1998.

Gillam, Martha Rascoe. Nags Head, N.C., 3 August 1998.

Gray, Carmen. Nags Head, N.C., 3 August 1998; Kitty Hawk, N.C., 26 July 2000.

Hall, Virginia Flora. Elizabeth City, N.C., 5 July 2000.

Howison, Betty Wales Silver. Raleigh, N.C., 28 July 1998; Nags Head, N.C., 27 July 2000.

Inglis, Frances Drane. Edenton, N.C., 9 August 2000.

Jones, Burton. Edenton, N.C., 21 June 2000.

Kittrell, Gilliam. Raleigh, N.C., 21 July 1998.

Nash, Florence. Durham, N.C., 25 April 2000.

Nash, Jaquelin Drane. Raleigh, N.C., 12 March 2000; Tarboro, N.C., 10 April 2000.

Nunemaker, Carl. Fall 2000.

Rascoe, Nancy Dawson. Nags Head, N.C., 3 August 1998; Hertford, N.C., 10 August 2000.

Rascoe, Peter, Jr. Nags Head, N.C., 3 August 1998; Hertford, N.C., 10 August 2000.

Rascoe, J. Peter, III. Nags Head, N.C., 2 August 1998 and 2 March 2000.

Read, Dorothy "Dee." Nags Head, N.C., 4 August 1998 and 27 July 2000; Hertford, N.C., 3 November 2000.

Reber, Charles. Nags Head, N.C., 2 March 2000.

Silver, John "Possum." Nags Head, N.C., 2 August 1998; Manteo, N.C., 3 March 2000.

Skinner, Tom. Nags Head, N.C., 3 August 1998 and 2 March 2000.

Spruill, Mary Elizabeth "Topsey." Colerain, N.C., 13 November 1999.

Stick, David. Kitty Hawk, N.C., 21 April 2000 and 10 October 2000.

Summerall, Lynn. Norfolk, Va., July 2000.

Tomlinson, Anne Buchanan. Raleigh, N.C., 15 January 2000; Nags Head, N.C., 27 July 2000.

Twine, Clayton. Elizabeth City, N.C., 20 April 2000.

Twine, Laura. Elizabeth City, N.C., 20 April 2000.

Twine, Mickey. Elizabeth City, N.C., 27 April 2000.

Twyne, Donnie. Manteo, N.C., 27 July 2000.

Wadsworth, Beulah. Edenton, N.C., 9 August 2000.

Wilson, Bill. Nags Head, N.C., 2 March 2000.

Winslow, Cecelia. Raleigh, N.C., 25 October 2000.

Winslow, Frank. Raleigh, N.C., 25 October 2000.

119

The E. R. Outlaw, Sr., Cottage was a one-story structure reportedly prefabricated from an older structure and shipped by steamer from Bertie County to Nags Head, where it was built in 1885. One of Nags Head's original thirteen, it now stands on the southern end of the Unpainted Aristocracy.

Photo by Drew Crawford Wilson

THE LAMB-MARTIN-STEWART-FOLK-PATTERSON COTTAGE, ONE OF NAGS HEAD'S ORIGINAL THIRTEEN, WAS SUPPOSEDLY MOVED FROM THE SOUND SIDE.

Photo by Drew Crawford Wilson

APPENDIX 2:
ORIGINAL OLD NAGS HEAD BEACH COTTAGES AND BATHHOUSE

The following appear as compiled by E. R. Outlaw, Jr. They are listed south to north.

EDWARD R. OUTLAW COTTAGE
4327 South Virginia Dare Trail
This cottage, built in 1885, is owned by the Worthington family.

JAMES GATLIN COTTAGE
4313 South Virginia Dare Trail
This cottage dates from 1868. Its original frame is the current High Cottage. Over the years, the Gatlin, Rascoe, Sawyer, Morrisette, Shepherd, Flora, Hayman, and High families have owned it.

SPIDER VILLA SHUT TIGHT AGAINST THE WINTER WINDS.

Photo by Drew Crawford Wilson

H. V. DUNSTAN COTTAGE
(ALSO CALLED THE DRANE COTTAGE)
IT STOOD AT 4303 SOUTH VIRGINIA DARE TRAIL.
This cottage was built around 1887. It was moved in 1963 and razed in 2000. The Dunstan, Drane, Graham, and Pruden families owned it.

SUMNER COTTAGE
(ALSO CALLED THE SUMNER-ROBINSON-GAITHER COTTAGE)
4215 South Virginia Dare Trail
This structure, built in 1869, has been owned by the Sumner, Robinson, and Gaither families.

OLD BATHHOUSE
Built sometime around 1870, this structure sat on a lot at 4131 South Virginia Dare Trail. It was moved to the road in 1935 and dismantled in 1938. It was owned by Dr. L. S. Blades.

E. F. LAMB COTTAGE
(ALSO CALLED THE LAMB-MARTIN-STEWART-FOLK-PATTERSON COTTAGE)
4121 South Virginia Dare Trail
This cottage was fashioned around a sound-side fishing shack moved to the oceanfront circa 1880. It has been owned by the Lamb, Martin, Folk, Stewart, and Patterson families.

THE WINSTON-WALES COTTAGE, SUPPOSEDLY BUILT FOR HENRIETTA FEARING IN 1869,
IS MORE LIKELY TO HAVE GRACED THE NAGS HEAD BEACHFRONT AROUND 1875.
IT IS THE SUMMER HOME TO BETTY WALES HOWISON OF RALEIGH.

Photo by Drew Crawford Wilson

WINSTON-WALES COTTAGE
4103 South Virginia Dare Trail
This cottage, built in 1869 or 1875, has been owned by the Fearing, Butt, Winston, Wales, Silver, and Howison families.

SPIDER VILLA
4049 South Virginia Dare Trail
This structure dates to 1859. It was formerly owned by the Griffin, Winston, and Drane families; it is currently owned by the Warren, Hoffman, and Miles families.

W. G. POOL COTTAGE
Constructed in 1855, this cottage was the first built on the oceanfront. It stood at 4031 South Virginia Dare Trail before it was destroyed by fire.

GEORGE D. POOL COTTAGE
(ALSO CALLED THE MACMULLAN COTTAGE)
4023 South Virginia Dare Trail
This cottage dates to 1866. It has been owned by the Pool family, Bradford and Company, the Turner family, the MacMullan family, and the Fisher family.

GRANDY-NIXON COTTAGE

4019 South Virginia Dare Trail

Constructed in 1866, this cottage was razed in October 2000 and replaced in 2001. It has been owned by the Grandy, Nixon, Oakey, Horton, and Read families.

WHEDBEE COTTAGE

4020 South Virginia Dare Trail

This cottage was built in 1868. It was formerly owned by the Overman, Bradford, Tunis, Old, and Whedbee families; it is currently owned by the Whedbee, Applewhite, and Sisco families. It was moved from the oceanfront to its current location in 1936.

PAILIN-SKINNER COTTAGE

4005 South Virginia Dare Trail

This cottage was built in 1886 and replaced in 1933.

MARTHA WOOD COTTAGE

4001 South Virginia Dare Trail

This cottage dates to around 1860. It has been owned by the Gurkin, Cobb, Grice, Wood, Fiveash, and Lester families.

THE PAILIN-SKINNER COTTAGE, SHUT TIGHT AGAINST THE FALL, WAS BUILT IN THE 1930s, REPLACING ONE BUILT IN THE 1880s FOR WILLIAM PAILIN OF ELIZABETH CITY.

Photo by Drew Crawford Wilson

TOWELS HANG FROM A LINE ON THE BACK PORCH OF THE BUCHANAN COTTAGE TODAY.
WHEN IT WAS BUILT BY S. J. TWINE IN 1936, THE COTTAGE, WITH ITS NINE BEDROOMS AND
BEAD-BOARD PANELING, WAS CONSIDERED THE FINEST HOUSE ON THE BEACH.

Photo by Drew Crawford Wilson

ACKNOWLEDGMENTS

When I was just a year old, my parents took me to spend my birthday in Nags Head, and I've loved it ever since. We returned to the Nags Head area every summer of my childhood. As we made our annual sojourn to watch the fishing boats dock at Oregon Inlet, we'd drive down the "slow road" past the Unpainted Aristocracy. Nags Head was full of intrigue for me back then, from my fascination with Virginia Dare and ghost and pirate tales to the mystery that surrounded the old gray cottage line. It was easy for me, a child given to daydreaming, to wonder what kind of families made these majestic places their homes.

Several summers ago, I was given the chance to find out. In writing a feature story for the Raleigh *News and Observer*, I discovered, like Catherine Bishir before me, that the history of Nags Head and the old cottages was far too compelling to be contained in a single story. The feature I wrote, "Time and Tide," appeared in the paper's *Sunday Journal* on August 23, 1998. It would take more than two years—and the help of many—to complete the book you hold in your hands. It is only part of the Nags Head story, centered on the cottages and the families who love them. But it is the part that captured me, and I hope I've told it well.

Much of the credit for the book's existence goes to Peter Rascoe, whose tireless passion for the history of Nags Head is infectious. It was Peter who first mentioned the idea of a book to me, and he continually encouraged me until the manuscript's completion. Peter committed countless hours to the project, tracking down sources and photographs, setting up interviews, and walking or driving the length of Cottage Row and the roads of eastern North Carolina with me. He opened many doors for me with Nags Head natives and cottage owners, convincing them that I could be trusted with their family histories. He used his talent for recalling the names and places and dates of North Carolina history to ensure my mistakes were few. In the process, he even learned a thing

or two he didn't know about a place he loves so much. Thank you, Peter. Without your extraordinary contribution, *Nags Headers* would never have been a book.

The development of *Nags Headers* was always driven by a force stronger than my own curiosity. Throughout my work, I had only to mention I was writing about Nags Head and stories found me. Just when I thought I had to end my research without an oral history I needed, I met Virginia Wood of Edenton, who introduced me to her mother, Virginia Flora Hall, then almost a hundred years old. Mrs. Hall had survived the hurricane of 1933, and hers was the story I'd been missing. There were countless times when similar serendipitous events occurred.

There are others who helped ensure *Nags Headers* is as accurate and complete as possible. My thanks go to Robert G. Anthony, old Halifax County friend and curator of the North Carolina Collection at the Wilson Library at UNC-Chapel Hill, who expertly read the manuscript for historical accuracy and provided supplements to my research, and to Catherine Bishir of the Survey and Planning Branch of the North Carolina Division of Archives and History, who read the manuscript with keen eyes and whose original work—"The Unpainted Aristocracy: The Beach Cottages of Old Nags Head," published in the *North Carolina Historical Review* in October 1977—inspired this book. Others who critiqued the book in different stages were Mary Cornatzer of the *News and Observer,* who fine-tuned my book proposal before I sent it to publishers; historian and author David Cecelski, who put in a good word for me; and Dawn Ronco, my "writer friend," who counseled me through two proposals and various setbacks but always believed *Nags Headers* would be published, even when I didn't. And, as always, I thank my husband, Rick, who listened even when he didn't want to and who read the manuscript too many times to count.

My thanks go to Laura Twine, S. J. Twine's niece, who opened up boxes of family photographs—as well as her family history—so I could learn more about the man whose work came to define Nags Head; to Sarah Downing and the staff of the Outer Banks History Center, who combed the files for just the right photographs for the book; to Don Pendergraft of the Museum of the Albemarle, for handling the Twine family photographs and documents with such care; to Fred Fearing and Frances Inglis, for sharing their private photo collections; to Drew Wilson, for capturing the essence of Nags Head in the many wonderful new images contained within the book; and to graphic artists Joe Wagner of Nags Head and Bill Drescher of Raleigh, without whose expertise in computer imaging technology Drew Wilson's digital photographs might not have arrived.

Two of David Stick's books, *The Outer Banks of North Carolina* and *The Ash Wednesday Storm*, proved particularly helpful to me. I am grateful to Stick for sharing his insight and his copy of the series of radio interviews called *The Nags Head Casino: Where the Good Times Rolled!* The series was produced by Lynn Summerall of WVOD in Manteo in 1989. Another book that proved of great use was Edward R. Outlaw, Jr.'s *Old Nags Head*.

I'm also indebted to Carolyn Sakowski of John F. Blair, Publisher, for her patience as I worked through some difficult times early in the publication process.

But my deepest appreciation goes to those who shared their family histories with me, for *Nags Headers* is indeed their story, not mine: the Silvers, the Dranes and Nashes, Virginia Flora Hall, Beulah Wadsworth, the Rascoes, the Buchanans and Couplands, Dee Read, Tom Skinner, Carmen Gray, the Twines, and all who opened up their memories to me and allowed me to put them to paper but are not mentioned here. I am humbled by the trust you placed in me. There are so many Nags Head families today that it would have been impossible to include all their stories in one book. The contributions of the Winslow family, Bill Wilson, Frances Drane Inglis, Burton Jones, and Mary Elizabeth "Topsey" Spruill, though not attributed, are sprinkled throughout the book in some form. There are many others who shared a tale or two with me while I was working on the book. I thank them all.

And to Rick, Meredith, and Graham, thanks for your patience with me, particularly in light of the many times I said, "As soon as I finish the book …" It's done now, so it's time to welcome me back.

⟢⟣

The book was made possible in part by funding from the Regional Artist Project Grant Program of the United Arts Council of Raleigh and Wake County.

The program is supported by funds from the North Carolina Arts Council (a state agency), the United Arts Council of Raleigh and Wake County, the War- ren County Arts Council, the Vance County Arts Council, the Franklin County Arts Council, and the Johnston County Arts Council.

A PATTERN OF ANGLES AND LINES, THE UNPAINTED ARISTOCRACY MARKS THE SKY DURING SUNSET.

Photo by Drew Crawford Wilson

INDEX